RIPE

Other books by Julia Moulden

We Are The New Radicals: A Manifesto for Reinventing
Yourself and Saving the World (McGraw-Hill, New York, 2008)

Green is Gold: Business Talking to Business About the
Environmental Revolution (HarperBusiness, 1991)

RIPE

Rich, Rewarding Work After 50

Your Guide to the Next, Best Phase of Your Career

A course in discovering passion, purpose and possibility at midlife

Julia Moulden

Dearest Louise,
May we have 50 years of
September dinners.
The best is yet to come!
Julia xo
March 2011

Printed in the United States of America.
First printing March 2011.

Library and Archives Canada Cataloging-in-Publication Data
978-0-9868260-0-9
Moulden, Julia 1956 Apr 2
Ripe: Rich, Rewarding Work After 50 ~ Your Guide to the Next, Best Phase of Your Career / by Julia Moulden

Visit juliamoulden.com

For my siblings Rick, Elizabeth and Jeff as they ripen

Contents

Introducing Ripe

Marilyn Robinson was a vivacious 61-year-old woman with a passion for two things—being a flight attendant and running marathons in cities around the world. On the day she retired, she walked through the empty cabin toward the front of the aircraft where her crew was assembled, ready to send her off with hugs and tears. Just before she reached her colleagues, Marilyn suddenly ducked into the washroom. Everyone laughed. But gradually it became clear that this wasn't a joke. She had locked herself inside the tiny cubicle and no amount of cajoling was going to bring her out. Security was called, and they carried Marilyn—kicking and sobbing—out of the plane and up the gangway into the terminal.

When I read about Marilyn in the paper, I realized she was acting out the intense frustration of an entire generation. Her tantrum was a howl of protest on behalf of the millions of Baby Boomers who aren't remotely ready to step aside and resent the calls for them to do so. Day by day, the resistance movement is growing. And our slogan might well be the one we used to protest the war in Vietnam, "Hell, no, we won't go!"

• • •

Society's prevailing view seems to be that beyond a certain age men and women suddenly become what I've dubbed "U3"— uninteresting, unattractive and basically useless. This perception is so widely held that most people don't give it a second thought. Consider how often we hear jokes about "senior moments." How seldom we see people older than 50 in advertisements for anything other than retirement planning, insurance or medication. Or, how frequently media reports on

1

the aging population are punctuated by high-temperature expressions such as "agequake" and "pension bomb."

When I started noticing this disturbing litany of messages, I was (in addition to being offended) curious. They certainly weren't describing me. At 53, I was enjoying a successful career as an author and career coach. In fact, I felt like I was just hitting my stride. I had accumulated a lifetime's worth of knowledge, skills and resources, and would describe myself as being at the top of my game. Was I the only one feeling this way?

I did what I've always done when confronted by a problem or puzzle: I raised my antennae. I started passing my daily dose of media through a filter. Could I find examples of men and women who, like me, were continuing to work? People who had broken away from this depressing groupthink?

I soon found lots of newsmakers who were on my wavelength. In just one week, I collected items on Baby Boomers such as Bill Gates, Oprah Winfrey, Meryl Streep and Al Franken; each could have chosen to retire but all were still hard at work. In the same week, golfer Tom Watson, 59, nearly won the British Open (Tiger Woods beat him by a mere 15 strokes). I also started to notice people older than me who were still in the game—men and women in their 60s (U.S. Vice President Joe Biden, actor Helen Mirren), 70s (primatologist Jane Goodall, actor Jack Nicholson), 80s (investor Warren Buffett, actor Betty White) and 90s (architect I.M. Pei, journalist Helen Thomas).

Clearly, I wasn't alone. Encouraged, I began to talk to people in my circle—friends and family, clients and colleagues, even my hairdresser. It was soon abundantly clear that Boomers were asking themselves the question, "What's next?" And, the answer for most was "work."

I turned to various sources of research and discovered they

supported my anecdotal findings. Some studies show as many as four out of five Baby Boomers will continue to work. McKinsey Global Institute, for instance, surveyed 5,100 American households in 2007 and found "Boomers want to continue working—as much as 85 percent say 'likely' and 40 percent say 'extremely likely'."

Something in the research made me think this was about more than simply continuing to work: Boomers reported they were now looking for stimulating new work and more satisfying ways of working.

I went back and looked at my notes again. Reading through them, some stories suddenly stood out from the rest. There was the management consultant who went back to school to earn a PhD in marine biology, the publisher who became a playwright, the serial entrepreneur who returned to revitalize his first company, and the academic who discovered a rich, new vein of research.

I realized something unprecedented was beginning to happen. This generation is not interested in traditional retirement. At this stage of our lives, we're looking for rich, rewarding work we can do with the confidence of professionals and the zest of beginners. We want to become what I call "ripe."

• • •

Is this the end of the road for the Baby Boom generation? Not by a long shot. We have every intention of resisting the arbitrary "best-before" date that is being imposed on us. And most of us fully intend to continue to work. In fact, we believe we're on the verge of the most important phase of our lives.

It's time for a radical rethink of our careers after 50. Let's get to work.

A World Ripe for Change

The pursuit of rich, rewarding work after 50 is a personal journey. However, our quest is fuelled not only by inner yearning but also by outside influences. It's not just you—the entire world view of aging, work and retirement is changing.

It wasn't long ago the goal at midlife was early retirement. Clever advertisers introduced the idea "Freedom 55" and we bought it. However, for most people, the pitch has become a pipe dream.

We've discovered that clocking out early just isn't viable. The majority of Baby Boomers simply can't afford it. As the Center for Retirement Research at Boston College in Massachusetts found, 60 percent of Boomers polled now intend to stay on the job past eligible retirement age. Why? Here's a clue from Canada: according to a 2010 survey commissioned by RBC Financial, four in 10 Canadians actually go into retirement with some form of debt (whether mortgages on their homes or new credit products).

Boomers aren't the only ones who are finding retirement costly—so does the world at large. Little wonder. When pension programs were first introduced (by German Chancellor Otto von Bismarck in 1889), the eligible age for benefits was 70 and the average lifespan was 45. With life expectancy around the globe increasing every year (it now hovers around 80) and pensions fixed anywhere from 60 to 65, it's no surprise that the prospect of pensioning off an entire generation for more than 20 years is looking a little pricey for everyone involved.

Add to this the fact that our planet is about to reach a watershed moment when there will be more people over 65 than under five and you begin to wonder who's going to fund it all.

Good question. As this book goes to print, US Steel workers in Hamilton, Ontario, have been locked out for three months. They've refused to sign a contract that would alter their pension plan and halt indexing on pensions for those already retired. (This local is an interesting microcosm of the world at large, where 900 employed workers must step up for 9,000 retirees.)

At the same time, a number of governments are considering moving the goal posts on retirement age—from the U.S. and the U.K. to France and Shanghai.

The economics are clear—more bodies in the workforce equals more income taxes and less strain on pension funds. RAND Corporation economist Nicole Maestas sums it up this way: "Further encouraging longer working lives may prove beneficial to both individuals and the nation as a whole." What kind of benefit are we talking about? McKinsey estimates higher rates of labour force participation as a result of longer careers in the U.S. could generate $12.9 trillion in GDP from now until 2035.

One way or another, members of the Boomer generation will likely find themselves working well into their 60s and beyond—whether for financial reasons, revised government regulations or, better yet, for the sheer love of it.

How To Use Your Guide to Ripening

Use this book to change your life.

It's a 12-week course in how to ripen—how to discover work with more passion, purpose and possibility.

Each week—or chapter—introduces essential concepts, inspiring examples and practical exercises designed to help you find your way.

Your journey begins with an overview of this big, new idea and what it takes to make the voyage. Then, you'll do some guided thinking and reflection. You'll learn about common ways to ripen and some of the endless variations. Finally, you'll discover how to choose your new role—and make a successful transition.

Use *Ripe* in the way that suits you best, given who you are, what you're looking for, and what's going on in your life right now.

You might do the Ripe Intensive: go through it a week at a time, reading each chapter and doing associated "spadework" exercises. Or, you could read *Ripe* through once to gain insight into this emerging movement, then return to the beginning to launch your own process of observation, experimentation and decision-making.

Regardless of how you use this guide, there are three things I'd like you to keep in mind.

First, the Ripe journey is not linear. You may find you want to go back and revisit earlier chapters with new eyes as you become more aware of who you are and what you want. With each pass, you'll add to your understanding of yourself and your future.

Second, my use of the word "weeks" is relative. How long it takes you to move through this process depends entirely on you and the competing demands for your time. Even if you do this as a Ripe Intensive, you may discover some weeks need to be stretched out over longer periods, while others can be condensed. Move through it at a pace that works for you.

Third, my intention was to create a simple, straightforward process. It's based on the work I've done over the past decade as a coach and consultant with clients on four continents—individuals and organizations in each field and every sector. *Ripe* is the next best thing to working together, one-on-one. (Naturally, I was my own guinea pig—developing these ideas and tools as I ripened. I'll share my own story from time to time.)

As you move along the path, remember you are not alone. Thousands of others are ripening along with you—whether on the other side of the planet or just down the street.

Support for your journey
This book is full of resources to help you ripen, some introduced in Week One, others as we journey together. As well, please visit my website—juliamoulden.com—to learn more about the latest thinking and tools, and to share more inspiring stories of Ripe pioneers like you.

WEEK ONE:
Are You Ripe for Change?

"Never retire! Do what you do and keep doing it. But don't do it on Friday. Take Friday off. Friday, Saturday and Sunday, go fishing, do sexual activities, watch Fred Astaire movies. Then from Monday to Thursday, do what you've been doing all your life, unless it's lifting bags of potatoes off the back of a truck. I mean, after 85, that's hard to do. My point is: live fully and don't retreat."
- Mel Brooks

What's on the horizon?
Shift your thinking about aging, work and retirement.

Passion, purpose and possibility after 50. Does that describe what you're looking for? Well, your timing couldn't be better. Something big is just beginning that will help your quest—how we think about this stage of life is undergoing dramatic change.

To call this recent shift in thinking unprecedented is not an exaggeration—20 years ago, we simply wouldn't be having this conversation. And, as odd as it may seem, the 65th Academy Awards are a perfect example of what I mean.

In 1992, the Oscars were groundbreaking. It was the first time a horror film won best picture ("The Silence of the Lambs") and the first time an animated film was nominated for that category ("Beauty and the Beast"). It was also the first time a senior citizen stole the show.

No easy feat given Billy Crystal was hosting. Crystal had the audience eating out of his hand, but when best supporting actor was called everything changed.

Jack Palance won. A tall, handsome, broad-shouldered guy with a full head of grey hair, he was clearly delighted as he bounded up the stairs to accept.

He made a crack about Crystal, his co-star in "City Slickers," and then he shifted gears. "You know, there are times when you reach a certain age plateau," he began, "when the producers talk about you and they say, 'Well, what do you think? Can we risk it? Can we do it? Can we use him?' The other guy says, 'I don't know, let's look at some younger guys, we can make them look older, but this one ...' They forget to ask you to go out there, and you do all these things. Like, for instance ..."

With that, this 73-year-old pushed off the podium and did something that is seared into our collective memory. He dropped to the floor and did a series of one-armed push-ups.

The audience roared its approval. My 30-something friends and I cheered from our ringside seats in the living room. "Not bad for an old guy," someone quipped, and we all laughed.

We Need to Work

In one wildly amusing scene, Jack Palance was doing much more than auditioning. He was sending a powerful message that's taken us two decades to decode.

Palance was telling us that we can keep working—long after the arbitrary age when we're supposed to stop. Yes, we change as the years go by, but we need not lose the things we treasure.

Mental decline, for instance, isn't inevitable. Scientists say there's no reason our brains have to degenerate as we age—they're "plastic" and can grow and develop just as they did when we were younger.

Physical decline isn't unavoidable either (as Palance proves). The physical changes we associate with aging—such as loss of strength, speed and agility—are not caused as much by the passing years as our sedentary lifestyle. Just as we need to continue to use our brains, we need to keep moving our bodies.

The truth is, as we age we actually improve in many ways. Enjoyment of life and happiness rise steadily after 50. We become more emotionally stable. And new capabilities and qualities emerge (we'll talk more about this later).

Part two of what Palance was saying? We must keep working. There is growing awareness that retirement isn't good for us. All of the longitudinal studies of lifespan show remaining "active and engaged" is essential to successful aging. Even the world's largest organization for retirees acknowledges that stopping work altogether may not be in our best interest. According to AARP (American Association of Retired Persons) studies show people who continue to work live longer—and in better health—than their retired peers.

The third part of Palance's message is we *should* keep working. We have a lifetime of experience under our belts and are at the height of our powers. Men and women in their 50s, 60s, 70s and beyond have much to contribute.

What Palance knew 20 years ago is just beginning to resonate with the rest of us. In response, the world at large—and the Baby Boom generation in particular—has begun to change the way it thinks about aging, work and retirement. For proof, we return to Hollywood—a perfect cultural barometer.

In 1992, Palance was the only nominee in his age group. Fifteen years later, a sea change happens. Suddenly, people older than 50 begin appearing in the "best" categories. Not some "old guy" who gets an Oscar because, well, it's time—these are people at the top of their game. In 2007, actors nominated for best-acting awards included Peter O'Toole, 74, Judi Dench, 72, Helen Mirren, 61, and Meryl Streep, 57. The same year, Martin Scorsese won the Oscar for best director—his first, at age 64.

By 2010, the tide had turned. The majority of nominees ranged from 50ish to 72, namely George Clooney, Colin Firth, Jeff Bridges, Meryl Streep, Helen Mirren and Morgan Freeman.

These are the Ripe pioneers. And they're not going anywhere.

Are You Ripe for Change?

When I first started talking about *Ripe*, people got the concept
—rich, rewarding work after 50—right away. Their faces lit up
with excitement and hope. Some of them even realized that
being 50-plus was about to become the place to be.
Philanthropic consultant Julia Howell blurted out, "I'm 47 ½!"
We laughed—when was the last time we appended half a year to
our ages? When was the last time we wanted to be older?

Like Julia, there are a growing number of us who look
forward to what's next. I've identified six distinct reasons
people decide to ripen. Does one of these sound like you?

"I'm successful and am looking for a new challenge."
He'd had a big career, culminating in a senior role at one of the
largest global companies. He told me he felt he'd learned
everything there was to learn, and done everything he could do.
"I'm at the top of my game and now I want to try something
new."

"I gave my life to others."
When they married, she had earned a degree from a good
university and was using her skills at a worthy not-for-profit. For
nearly 30 years, she'd stayed home to raise their family. At 53,
she was climbing the walls. "I made a conscious choice," she
told me. She was glad she'd been there for her kids, "but it's my
turn now."

"I realized I need to work."
He'd done everything right, but lost his life savings when the
financial crisis hit. He told me he was over the shock of having
to continue to work—and he really wanted to shift his view of

the situation. "Now I want to believe this really can be the most satisfying period of my career. Could I actually *want* to work?"

"This road has come to an abrupt end."
"I'm lost in a dark wood with no way out," he mumbled, slumped in his chair. A successful venture capitalist for decades, at 56 he had become yesterday's man. Effectively pink slipped in his prime, he was unmoored and miserable.

"I haven't lived up to my potential."
She felt she got off on the wrong foot professionally, and moving countries repeatedly to follow her husband's career meant hers never quite got on track. "Do you think we have second chances?," she asked. "Is there still time?"

"I retired and want to go back to work."
Walter Cronkite was publicly candid about the fact that retirement was the worst decision he'd made—he called it "statutory senility." Many people enjoy the break at first, but then are eager to find their way back in. This includes those who were nudged into retirement—involuntarily, sometimes by their spouses—and have come to regret it.

The impetus for your journey could be any of these realizations. But something else will mark its official start—a decision to wholeheartedly reject the notion that it's time to stop working. That may sound minor (or obvious) but it is absolutely essential. Shifting our perspective—deciding that we're ripe for change—is the cornerstone of the foundation on which our new work will be built.

• • •

So far, we've been talking mostly about high-profile Ripe pioneers. In the weeks to come, you're going to meet ordinary people who are doing extraordinary things at 50, 65, 80 and beyond. And each of them is eager to help you find your way—without having to resort to push-ups!

Read on to learn about the tools you'll pick up now that will help guide your journey. (If you haven't already done so, please take a look at "How to Use Your Guide to Ripening" on page 5.) And then, when you're ready, dive into Week Two.

Journal

A journal is every traveller's best friend. It's a recording device, a place to keep track of important details—new ideas and observations, meaningful quotes and milestones. It is also your friend—a source you can turn to (and return to) to share what's really going on inside of you. Over time, it will become your coach or teacher. As you reread it, you'll discover insights, see how you're changing and how far you've come.

In fact, here's your first exercise. Are you ripe for change? Write about how you're feeling at this moment, whether you feel ready for the journey, and why (or why not). You might like to try the Ripe checklist.

✅	The Ripe Checklist can help you decide if you're ready to ripen. How many of these statements apply to you?
	I resist the idea that I'm past my "best-before" date.
	I feel that I have more to do and lots to give.
	I feel confident, experienced, mature. I'm just getting started!
	I keep thinking to myself, "Now it's my turn!"
	I'm ready to try something new, to be stretched.
	I'm looking for a new passion, new purpose.
	I'm curious about the world, and want to play a part in it.
	Retirement gives me the willies.
	I'm burning to do the things I've always wanted.
	I recognize that something is rising up inside of me. Something I can't ignore.
	I want to explore what comes after 50.
	I can't wait to see what's next!
	I'm looking for role models for the next phase of my career.
	I'm looking for ideas.
	I feel a resurgence of energy.
	I'm mid-career, not midlife.
If you've checked any of these statements, you're ready to begin your ripening journey.	

Spadework

Each week I'll ask questions and suggest exercises that will help deepen what you're learning and discover what it means to you. Here's what I want you to think about now.

1. Do you have some idea of the work you'd like to do? If yes, what is it? And how do you feel contemplating it now? If you don't have any idea, how does that make you feel?

2. Do you see Ripe role models around you? In your community? In leadership roles? In history? Who are they—and what can you learn from them?

3. What are you most afraid will happen—or not happen—on this journey? What is your greatest wish for yourself now? What is your greatest fear?

4. The Ripe Pledge. You're embarking on a significant voyage—one that requires courage and commitment. Take a few moments to write a pledge for yourself, whether one line or 10, that spells out your dedication to this path. Say it aloud. And come back to it from time to time.

At any point in the journey, you can go back and review earlier weeks.

W e e k **1** • 2 • 3 • 4 • 5 • 6 • 7 • 8 • 9 • 10 • 11 • 12

Are You Ripe for Change? Reject the notion it's time to step aside.

Week One in Review

- Jack Palance at the Oscars: His one-armed push-ups were more than an audition for this 73-year-old actor. He was sending a three-part message.

- First, we can keep working. Decline isn't inevitable—and we actually make gains.

- Second, we must keep working. Retirement isn't good for us.

- Third, we *should* keep working. We are at the top of our game and have much to offer.

- Six common reasons people take the ripening journey:

  "I'm successful and looking for a new challenge."
  "I gave my life to others and now it's my turn."
  "I'd like to shift my thinking from having to work to *wanting* to."
  "This road has come to an abrupt end."
  "I haven't lived up to my potential."
  "I retired and want to return to work."

WEEK TWO:
Prepare For Your Journey

"To dare is to lose one's footing momentarily. Not to dare is to lose oneself."
- Soren Kierkegaard

What's on the horizon?
Learn about the essentials that aid the road to ripening.

Rona Maynard, 61, from magazine editor to author to work in progress

"I left Chatelaine in 2004. When I did, I said publicly that I didn't have anything else lined up and my goal was to surprise myself. I was perceived to be at the top of my game and wanted to leave that way—I didn't want to overstay my welcome, get stale in my job. It felt great to do it like that. I thought, 'I am the kind of person who can be an active creator of my life.'

And then there was thunderous silence. I knew I wasn't going to just sit on the couch and read Emily Dickinson for the rest of my life. Readers had been asking for a book, and I had an idea that I might write my autobiography. My life took on shape again, and the book became an all-consuming passion.

You have to remember that I'd been working in magazine journalism all my career and I'd been writing to length, to assignment, to a particular audience. So I had tremendous trouble in the beginning writing anything longer than column length. I thought, I'm a good writer, I should be able to do this. But I would start writing and at the end of 800 words, I'd think, well, what's next? It took me a long time to figure out how to write more discursively. It was incredibly liberating when it came.

I recognized that my bond with readers was rooted in my personal journey from underachiever to dynamic leader. For years I battled shyness and chronic depression. I struggled to reconcile the pressures of my career with my other roles as mother, wife, daughter and friend. I never set out to change other people's lives, but that is what began to happen when I wrote from the heart about changing my own life.

Once the book [My Mother's Daughter, McClelland & Stewart] came out I had a huge sense of let down. I'd had this big passion and now what?

Everyone is talking about how exciting it is to change careers, but no one says what it's like to be between chapters. Which is where I am now.

Having been through this process once before, I know I'll find my way again. For now, I'm in a state of quiet alertness. I'm out there meeting people, feeding my head—it's something you have to do when you don't have colleagues because you can't do it all by yourself. I feel as if my brain and psyche are gearing up for something."

W hen I share stories of Ripe pioneers like Rona Maynard with friends or at dinner parties, someone usually declares the Ripe experience is a gift given magically to a fortunate few. Others insist it happens naturally, pointing out "fruit falls from the tree when it's ripe!" The reality is, as Rona discovered, ripeness is neither a happy accident nor simple good fortune—it must be cultivated and nurtured.

Ask any farmer. These seasoned professionals know the right mix of sun, water and nutrients will produce the perfect fruit, and do everything possible to ensure a good harvest. This week is about creating the conditions that will encourage your successful ripening. What blend of insight and care will grow the plump, juicy pear that falls off the stem into your eager hands?

In taking the Ripe Pledge last week, you picked up the first of the tools you'll need for your journey—these will support you as you move through the challenges and savour the joys that lie ahead.

Now, let's talk about other essentials you'll need to put in place before your journey gets fully underway: time, space and support.

Time

Few people need to be convinced that finding the time to make this journey is mission critical—or that this might actually be difficult to achieve in our constantly-connected, overly-scheduled lives.

But I'll say it anyway, because you need to make the case to yourself and your loved ones and any others on whom changes to your regular routine will have an impact. You need time. Time for you and your ripening journey. Time when you can completely unplug; when you will not be disturbed. And time that you will defend against all invaders.

Rick Archbold, a busy author and editor, decided if he wanted to ripen, he would have to establish a routine for himself. "If you think you are going to do this when the inspiration strikes or when you 'find' the time, forget it. You are not going to get anything done. You have to create a ritual, set aside a certain amount of time per day. I would take the phone off the hook each morning, usually for about three hours, and not check email."

I'm with Rick. When I was writing this book, I told my regular clients (and friends and family) I wouldn't be available from 6 a.m. to noon each day. I explained to them it was my book writing time, and told myself I would vigorously protect it. Most people readily agreed.

How much time? That depends on you, your current work, and how fast you want to make this journey. I. Garrick Mason, a consultant and publishing entrepreneur, rises at 4:15 a.m. so he has time for himself before the demands of the day encroach. Others prefer to do it in increments.

Time of day is worth considering, too. You'll notice Rick, Garrick and I all work earlier in the day. We do this partly because we've learned that—like exercise—if we don't get to our work first, we won't have time or energy to do it at all. Plus, we've discovered (and research backs this up) as we age, we are sharper in the morning. This isn't true for everyone, of course. Only you will know when your mind and body are at their best. Snag some of that time for your ripening journey.

For those who can swing it—and afford it—long stretches of time away give us the opportunity to really devote ourselves to ripening. In my last book about rethinking what we do for a living (*We Are The New Radicals*, which explores how our work can become the way we "give back"), I shared Rocco Rossi's story, how he went from the corporate fast track to the non-profit world. In the intervening years, he's become a serial re-inventor, finding new ways to put the skills he's acquired to work. In 2010, he decided to run for mayor of Toronto. It was a difficult race with lots of surprises and upsets. About a month before election day, when his poll numbers weren't looking good, Rossi decided to withdraw from the race. I sent him an email admiring his courage, compassion and grace under pressure—and encouraged him to give himself time to mourn and rest. He replied that he was off to the Camino de Santiago (a pilgrimage path across Spain) to consider what he might do next.

Clearly, in a perfect world, that would be ideal for all of us—to truly escape from our lives and have a chance to reflect, recharge, and come back renewed and ready to ripen. (In fact, I explore the idea of what I've come to think of as a "gap year for grown-ups" in Week Twelve.)

Space

"A room of one's own" is how author Virginia Woolf put it. She was talking about what women writers need, but the same holds true for people who want to ripen. We need somewhere comfortable and safe where we are free to focus our attention on this process.

What kind of space? That depends on you. I've worked with clients who set aside a room in their homes where they can close the door and work in peace, and those who prefer the sanctuary of the bubble bath. Some people work well in noisy cafés. Others think best in motion. Entrepreneur Vicki Saunders got her idea for an online social networking tool, Zazengo, while flying across the Atlantic. "I spend 30 percent of my time in the air," she told me, adding it gives her the space she needs. "As soon as I settle into my seat, I put on my 'cone of silence.' It's the best place for me to work bar none."

You may also need different kinds of space at different points in your journey. Noisy, crowded public spaces may be good when you are simply reflecting, for instance, but not that helpful when you're imagining. Many people engaged in the Ripe process spoke about finding the psychic elbow room they need in the natural world. Lee Weinstein, who fled corporate life to open his own public relations firm, found his answers came more easily when he was in the great outdoors. "Getting outside, being in nature, hiking—all of that was really essential," he said. "Some of my greatest epiphanies came when I was sitting next to the Salmon River in Oregon."

Support

Winston Cahill retired from the civil service at 64. Widowed a few years earlier, he decided to move "home"—returning to the small town where he grew up, half a continent away from the city where he and his wife raised their family. In many ways, it was a smart move—he was able to plug into the community, volunteering and enjoying an immediate social life (the only bachelor for miles!). But he wasn't happy being retired, and we worked together to help him find his way back into the workforce. One day, he had an important insight. "I realized the people in this community really believe in 'U3'," he told me (referring to an expression I use to describe how the world sees us after 50, "unattractive, uninteresting and basically useless"). "They think 50 is old and 60 is positively over the hill," he said. In contrast, his friends in the city were still in the game in their 70s.

It's lovely to imagine that we'll get all the support we need to ripen from our family and friends. And this may happen for you. Michelle and Tal Bevan, for instance, decided to leave the corporate world at the same time, and were able to actively support one another's ripening. Most people, though, find the decision to undertake this journey is met with a range of responses—from curious to openly hostile.

Discussing the ripening journey with those closest to us is essential. You might, for instance, share the fact it's a process that takes time and requires commitment, but the outcome (greater satisfaction derived from your work) makes the investment worthwhile. David Simms, a former consultant who is now chairman of a global micro-finance organization, told me he wouldn't have considered saying yes to his new role—a full-time commitment with lots of travel—unless it was a family decision.

"If my wife hadn't been equally committed, I wouldn't have done it."

What else can we do to get the support we'll need? We can enlist people to actively assist us. I recommend a team approach —a Ripe Circle (for support) and a Ripe Kitchen Cabinet (for advice). Together, they will help you act with clarity, conviction and courage.

• Ripe Circle

I get lots of energy being with people who understand me and support my work. Suddenly it's not just about being a crazy solo traveller cutting through dense underbrush, feeling exhausted and lost. I have a cheering section, a pit crew and a group hug.

No matter how you describe it, the intention is the same: your Ripe Circle is your support group. They will listen and cheer you on. They will pick you up when you fall, and help you lean toward hope and away from despair. More than that, they will keep you moving toward the summit when every cell in your body is screaming it's time to give up. "Some days, all I could think about were the reasons why what I was doing was completely useless, like 'the world does not need another children's book,'" blogger and aspiring author Rosanne Freed said. "My Ripe Circle told me 'Don't give up!' and for that I kiss their feet."

Social innovator David Simms shared his favourite metaphor with me. "Canada geese fly in formation for a reason," he said. "It allows them to go faster, the lead goose breaks the force of the wind and the other geese honk to encourage the ones in front!"

The members of your Ripe Circle may be on the journey, too—and you will support one another. Or they may simply be wise and compassionate companions, those who've been down this path or hope to some day follow you. Choose them well: their job is to love you. (Honk!)

• Ripe Kitchen Cabinet

You'll also need tough love. And this is where your Ripe Kitchen Cabinet comes in. These advisors will help you think critically about what you're going to do next. Choose them with equal care. You need just the right mix of ingredients—people with different expertise and perspectives. (The number isn't important. You might want 10 people at the table or just one trusted individual.)

Much as I'd love to take credit for the phrase "kitchen cabinet," it's not mine. I first heard it from entrepreneur Lee Weinstein, and I laughed with delight when he shared it. Lee's own cabinet helped him think through what he would do and how to make the transition. I asked him to describe his team. "I put together a wonderful group of advisors with divergent backgrounds and opinions. A college friend who freelances, another friend who works for a big PR firm, and a dear friend who'd run the career-planning department at a local college. Together, they were the voice of reason. They asked hard questions that were really useful."

My own Ripe Kitchen Cabinet is large and informal—I have weekly conversations with half a dozen advisors I've worked with for several years. They represent a wide range of leaders from various sectors, including technology, human resources, communications and social media, non-profit and government. Knowing they've got my back makes me feel incredibly secure.

What To Expect When You're Ripening

Each Ripe journey is unique. Yet much of what we experience is common to all our paths.

For instance, none of us knows how, where or when our journey will end. You might stay on the same career path (becoming what I call a "Master") or head in a new direction (a "Pathfinder"). As you'll discover, not knowing is an essential part of the process. At this stage, it's important to stay open to the possibilities.

What else might you expect? To feel like you're on an emotional roller coaster. Remember what it feels like to fall in love? Some days you're over-the-moon happy, half out of your mind with joy—and ever so certain you've made the right choice. At other times, you may feel bored or frustrated, anxious or uncertain—and you may begin to doubt your choice. Writer Rick Archbold says it was true for him. "On my good days, I would say, 'How great is this!?' And on my bad days, I'd say, 'What have you got to show for it?'"

You are, above all, vulnerable. In declaring your goal—to ripen—you have exposed yourself. And doing so means people will be watching closely. Sure, some will wonder if you're going to fall flat on your face or lose everything. Far more, however, will be watching to see what you do in the (perhaps undeclared) hope they can some day follow suit.

You're also charting new territory in terms of process and outcome. With a traditional career, we know—more or less— what's required to get there and what "there" means. We set a goal and power our way toward it—degree, intern, junior, associate, partner. In contrast, Ripe pioneers often have to find their own way and create unprecedented roles. While the Ripe process is designed to be as simple and straightforward as possible, your journey may be anything but. It requires thought and analysis, exploration and reflection, courage and persuasion.

Plus, as mentioned, the journey is not a linear one, from point A to point B. I think of it as circular, and here's what I mean. You might find, as you move through the book, you'll want to revisit other chapters, review them and rethink them. As you learn more about yourself and as your future begins to take shape, you may want to cross the same terrain over again, seeing it from new angles with fresh eyes.

You'll soon discover that ripening is not magic at all, but hard work fuelled by revelations. Above all, it's about steady, joyful, meaningful movement toward a new future. This week sets things in motion. As you move, you'll discover things begin to propel your journey in unexpected—and completely delightful—ways.

Bon voyage!

Journal

• Time

What can you do to make room in your day and week? How can you find time to ripen? What do you need to give up or postpone? And, how will you protect this time?

• Space

What kind of space is right for you? Do you work best in a comfy chair at home? Do you like the energy of public spaces? Think about what you need. And, begin to create it now.

• Support

Have you discussed your interest in ripening with your loved ones? Who might be part of your supportive Ripe Circle? Your Ripe Kitchen Cabinet of advisors? Reach out to them and be candid about what you need. You'll be delighted to hear their responses.

Spadework

1. Ripe Principles. In Week One you took the Ripe Pledge, one of the first steps on your ripening journey. Now, let's take time to think about the principles that will guide your journey—what's important to you, what will help you stay on course, and what you can come back to when you begin to feel doubt or despair.

Consultant I. Garrick Mason told me when he's working with young recruits, he often offers this advice: "Achieving an important goal in your career is like swimming across a stretch of open water to a lighthouse. The wind is up and every few strokes you're hit by a wave. Occasionally, a wave moves you toward your goal, but most push you away from it. You can't avoid waves; what you can do, though, is pull your head up after every breaker, find that lighthouse again and correct your course. If you keep swimming with your head down, you'll reach land eventually—but miles from where you were headed."

Your Ripe Principles will help keep you headed for the lighthouse. Here are some suggestions to get you started. Keep going until you've got a set of principles that feels right to you.

Your principles could be statements of fact:
- People of all ages should be encouraged to develop and contribute throughout their lives.
- Everyone has the potential to ripen.
- There are thousands of others on this path with me.

Or they might be affirmations:
- I am at the top of my game and have much to contribute.
- I am creating the conditions that will help me ripen.
- I will find rich, rewarding new work.

2. Who or what stands in the way of your ripening? What can you do to counteract this energy?

⟳ At any point in the journey, you can go back and review earlier weeks.

W e e k   1 • **2** • 3 • 4 • 5 • 6 • 7 • 8 • 9 • 10 • 11 • 12

Prepare for Your Journey - Create time, space and support for yourself.

Week Two in Review

- People think ripening either happens naturally or is a gift given magically to a fortunate few.

- In fact, ripening must be nurtured. It's hard work fuelled by revelations.

- You can create conditions that will encourage your ripening.

- Time: you need a specified amount of time each week, uninterrupted.

- Space: you need a place to work in comfort and privacy.

- Support: you need two teams – one for support (Ripe Circle), the other for advice (Ripe Kitchen Cabinet).

- Every Ripe journey is different, but you can expect both highs and lows.

- The trick is to keep moving. Action leads to the unexpected – and results.

WEEK THREE:
Review

"Better late than early."
- Orson Welles

What's on the horizon?
Look back and re-examine your career to date.

Ira Levine, 63, from university dean to university dreamer

"The year after I stepped down as dean of communications and design, I started teaching full time, which was new to me. I enjoyed it, especially interacting with the students, but I soon realized I needed something more.

I was asked to substitute for another department chair, so I went back into administration for a while. But, once again, I soon realized—as a temporary position stretched into two years—I really didn't need to continue doing work of that nature, either.

In the back of my mind I had this idea there was a need for collaborative work across sectors at the university. So, I proposed a project that would create a program of study in what I call 'creative industries' to link media, design, publishing and traditional cultural industries such as performing arts, visual arts and music. This new program would connect these industries to the new knowledge-based economy.

It had—and still has—no parallel anywhere. No prototype of any kind. I was starting with a blank piece of paper. And anyone who's been a dean will tell you that's a rare privilege. To start from scratch.

Having led the university through a transition already, I felt uniquely qualified. This was a big undertaking. It involved soliciting the support of many partners within the university, getting input from experts, ensuring the support of the government, both in terms of base funding and capital, as we needed to design and construct a new building to house this new venture.

It's heavily strategic and requires all of the experience I've had as a dean to make a success of it. Plus, I've always been one of those people who understood this university's finances—in addition to my strong strategic bent, I have a very good financial sense.

I'd done many of the elements of this role before, but nothing on quite this scale or with this degree of originality. As a target of my creative energy, it has been all consuming. And it's undoubtedly the most important work I've done, too. Helping a university achieve its goals is one thing, and I'm really proud of that contribution. But this, well, this is about imagining what the world will be like in 10 or 20 years and helping to create it. Who has the chutzpah to suggest what employment opportunities look like that far out? To prepare students for jobs that don't currently exist?"

Ira Levine began his ripening journey by looking back on his years with the university. It may seem counter-intuitive to start this way—"This is about my future, isn't it?"—but it's actually ideal.

To begin with, a review will give you energy. It feels great to remember where we've been, what we've done, who we've met. To make imaginary eye contact with the young person we once were, and fully appreciate what has gone into making us who we are today. Secondly, a review will give you vital information. I sometimes describe the ripening process as an equation: [experience + passion = ripening]. This week, you're filling in the first part of the formula. What is your experience? Of what, exactly, are you a master?

At this stage, your Ripe Kitchen Cabinet of advisors should be in full swing. Book a session with them to review what you're doing. And invite them to offer their informed perspective and insight on where you've been and how it might relate to your future. It can be wonderfully revealing to see ourselves as others see us.

Story

Let's begin by sketching out your career from when and where it began to where you are today. This isn't simply about updating your resume or your LinkedIn profile. It's more than a simple list of organizations, titles and responsibilities. You're going to tell the story of your working life: experiences, people, places—everything it took to build the professional capacity you now have.

Every time I interviewed a Ripe pioneer for this book—or whenever I've had a conversation with someone I wanted to profile in my *Huffington Post* column—I began with a review. I do it casually, generally asking for "a thumbnail sketch of your career." One of the secrets of a successful interview is to get people talking, to loosen them up and encourage them to move away from prepared answers and familiar territory. And it works. People start chatting away, and as their story pours out magical things begin to happen. First, a sense of pride emerges. I can actually hear the satisfaction in their voices as they go through the long list of things they've done. And then the interview really gets underway, and I let it go wherever it takes us. (Of course, now that I've shared my secret, I'll have to change tactics!)

The same thing will happen to you. There's something about recounting our past as if it were a story that helps us see our working lives in a new way. Weaving a narrative, we begin to see the threads that run through our careers and the patterns that emerge. "You know, I've never put it all together quite like this," said John Elkington (a consultant we'll meet in Week

Nine). "The things that seemed apparently unconnected were all, in the end, relevant."

The Ripe review can be powerfully satisfying if you've been successful, and even more so if you're feeling disenchanted, restless or anxious. Does that surprise you? It's human nature to focus on what we haven't done. As physicist and chemist Marie Curie put it, "One never notices what has been done; one can only see what remains to be done." Whether we judge our careers as successes or failures, we have learned much more than we appreciate.

Which is why, once you've written your career story (instructions appear at the end of this chapter), I want you to pause for a moment. The reason? I want you to revel in it. Congratulate yourself on having reached this age and done all that. Remember what it was like to land a particular job, make a difficult presentation or cash that bonus cheque. Take time to savour your lifetime of experience. You've earned it.

Skills

Once upon a time, people were their jobs: butcher, baker, candlestick maker. And these were their jobs for life. Although this is no longer the case, many people feel shackled by their job description. Val Fox, director of a digital-media incubator, who has seen this with friends and colleagues, describes it this way, "It's difficult for people to see beyond the wrapper they put around their job—they associate with a title rather than what they do."

How does someone break free from their self-imposed stereotype so they can move forward? By deconstructing what they do and framing it as a set of what are known as "transferable skills." And then, creating a portfolio of these skills to take along with them wherever they go.

The concept of transferable skills is one of the most important ideas to have emerged in career-planning circles in recent years, and it's caught on because it's smart, simple and it works. (See the following standardized list).

Transferable skills

Attitude/personality
Client/customer orientation
Communication
Drive/tenacity
Financial acumen
Leadership
People skills
Problem solving
Strategic thinking
Teamwork
Time management

Ripe pioneers understand it's essential to identify your skills—a process you've begun by telling the story of your career. As you read the narrative you've written, compare it to the standardized list of transferable skills. You'll be able to spot capabilities that can move with you. Debbie Dimoff, a serial reinventor who has worked in senior roles in technology, banking and professional services told me, "I have a basic tool kit that goes everywhere I do—I communicate, I write, I get people moving in the same direction."

For some Ripe pioneers, the skill set they needed was straightforward. Ira Levine, whose story appears at the beginning of this chapter, was quite clear he had what it took. As he mentioned, "having led this university through a transition already, I felt uniquely qualified." Plus, he knew the new role would require "all of the experience I've had as a dean" as well as his "very good financial sense."

But what about Ripe pioneers who use their skills in a completely different arena? Laurie Orlov left a consulting job to open her own firm. Before she made the move, she thought carefully about whether her capabilities matched the challenge before her. "I knew technology. I knew how to do research. I knew how to analyze." She also considered how she would use her skills to do things that were new to her. "I knew how to communicate, so I reasoned that I could convince people who were interested in what I had to say to actually pay me to say it!"

I was delighted to discover this whole notion of transferable skills is happening everywhere, not just in the executive suite or among the creative class. For instance, when a group of middle-aged, Canadian assembly-line workers were laid off from General Motors, they started their own company, manufacturing "new" cars from old parts. A group of 50-something employees in the Netherlands who were unwilling to see Polaroid die, long after investors had given up on the company, brought it back to life in 2010 (and no doubt felt completely vindicated when the classic Polaroid camera made O Magazine's list of favourite things that July). In Poland, a group of out-of-work ship builders in their 50s and 60s decided to pool their resources and create a new firm—and their own future—weld by weld.

Strengths

This is the time of life to play to our strengths.

Our "strengths" are our natural talents. What we do with ease. With pleasure. And when we bring these strengths to work with us, it's thrilling—we feel engaged, fully alive, and often lose track of time.

Many Ripe pioneers spoke passionately about their strengths. Kelly McDougald, a former technology executive who now leads an executive placement firm, says, "I've always seen myself as a problem-solver—I really like to find ways to engage a diverse group of stakeholders and figure out how to grow a business." Entrepreneur Lee Weinstein told me, "I love learning and changing. I'm always trying new things."

Do you know what your strengths are? Again, your career story may help you identify them. There are also tools that can help. Drs. Martin Seligman and Christopher Peterson, working with the VIA Institute in the U.S., identified six character strengths common to every culture around the world: wisdom, courage, humanity, justice, temperance and transcendence. And they've developed a questionnaire everyone can use to assess their own. (More about this web-based tool in the Journal section.)

You could also ask the people in your life—including your Ripe Circle and Ripe Kitchen Cabinet—to help you pinpoint your strengths. Ask them to share what they've observed and how you've put your natural talents to good use.

As you move through the ripening process, keep thinking about your strengths and skills, and how they might be useful in your new role.

· · ·

By the end of Week Three, you might be feeling pretty good. There will likely be a new spring in your step. You're starting to realize you've got a vast reservoir of valuable experience at your fingertips, and a growing sense of how you might be able to make use of it in the years to come.

It's natural when feeling this good to want to skip ahead and answer the question that brought you to the ripening path: "What's next?" If you do have an answer and are eager to get started, then go for it. But I must tell you when this happens with my clients, I gently recommend they hold off a little.

Human nature dictates when we're faced with a problem or quandry, we think we need to solve it immediately. As a result, most of us feel the pressure to move quickly into new work. As he was making the transition from corporate life to self-employment, Lee Weinstein told me he'd watched his peers struggle with this very thing. "People kept saying 'I've got to get a job, I've got to get a job.'"

If you can hold off a little longer, you'll see there is much more to discover. Because this journey isn't just about reconnecting with what you do, but (re)discovering who you are.

Journal

• Story

Pretend I'm interviewing you. Tell me the story of your career. Where did you go to school? What did you study? What was your first job? What kinds of things have you done? Where have you worked? Who did you meet? What were the high points and low? Do you remember a time when you couldn't wait to get out of bed in the morning?

Just keep writing. Note anything and everything that comes. And don't worry if the line between work and life blurs—we'll use the "life" bits later in this process. And make sure you leave lots of room—no doubt you'll want to add to it later (you're going to be coming back to this exercise as memories float to the surface. "Oh, yeah, remember when ...?").

I've done this with coaching clients, but in a slightly different way. Before my client arrives, I attach a huge piece of paper to the longest wall of my consulting room (you can buy long rolls of paper at art supply stores). When she arrives, we draw a long line, and add a dot for each year. Then she fills in the blanks—writing jobs and memories all across the wall. (I love this method because we can come back to it and build on it in the weeks to come.)

Some people have great difficulty writing. When this happens, we simply record their work story electronically instead. If this is this case for you, try this option, then listen and take notes as you play it back.

Don't labour over the words themselves. This isn't about style but content. Just write. Do free writing—move your hand across the page for a set period of time without stopping. Or try using bullet-points to get you started, then add a memory to each.

And if you haven't had a traditional career—if you've worked inside the home, for instance—write about that, too. It's part of your lifetime of experience, and you'll be surprised by the skills and strengths you'll be able to identify.

• Skills

Once the story of your career is complete, read through it to identify your skills. Then, while referring to the standardized list of transferable skills (on page 41), pinpoint the ones that apply to you.

If you have difficulty assessing your skills or strengths you might want to invite trusted friends and associates, including those in your Ripe Circle and Ripe Kitchen Cabinet, to help. Ask them what talents they've observed, and how they've seen you put them into action.

• Strengths

Go over your story once again. This time identify your strengths.

If you've never done the VIA Strengths Survey developed by Drs. Martin Seligman and Christopher Peterson, take the time to do it now. It will help you identify your five greatest qualities. <viacharacter.org>

Spadework

1. Describe what it feels like to be you, right here, right now.

2. Five things. List five things you've loved about your work. Then, list five things you've been praised for. And don't stop at five—if there are more (of course there are!) keep going.

3. Five people. List five people you've loved working with. Five people you admire. Once you've done this, move to the next part of the exercise below.

Now, is there anyone on either list you'd secretly like to be? Why? What is it about this person that appeals? What other clues are waiting for you to discover about these people? Do they tell you about the types of people you'd like to work with, for instance? The sort of teams you'd like to be part of? What else?

At any point in the journey, you can go back and review earlier weeks.

W e e k   1 • 2 • ❸ • 4 • 5 • 6 • 7 • 8 • 9 • 1 0 • 1 1 • 1 2

Review - Look back at what you've done and learned

Week Three in Review

- We begin our ripening by looking back—remembering what we've done that makes us feel good and provides vital information. Make eye contact with the young person you once were.

- The ripening process can be seen as an equation: [experience + passion = ripening].

- Tell the story of your career—when and where it started, experiences, people and places along the way.

- Create a portfolio of transferable skills—capabilities you can carry forward into your new role.

- Assess your strengths—your natural talents and how you've used them.

- Revel in the vast reservoir of experience you've created.

- Try not to jump into the first job that comes along. Give yourself time to really explore all the options.

WEEK FOUR:
Reflect I

"Now, aged 50, I'm just poised to shoot forth quite free, straight and undeflected my bolts whatever they are."
- Virginia Woolf

What's on the horizon?
Consider what you need and what's important now.

Lisa Bayne, 58, from creative director to CEO of creative company

"I went to art school and became a clothing designer for large manufacturers. In the late '80s, when retailers realized they needed to start designing their own clothing, I launched an in-house design department for Eddie Bauer. I was there for 14 years and, by the end, was overseeing a huge team of designers.

And then it all blew up. Business was terrible. I knew I was on the way out. I was 49, the sole breadwinner in our family, with a son in his junior year of high school and a daughter in the eighth grade.

I was recruited for two very different positions, and chose the smaller firm. We moved our family from Seattle to California–from our dream home to half the house for twice the money. I went from running a department of 130 people to working for a company with 100 people in total. I turned 50 and hit menopause. Throughout, I was hell-bent on proving I could do it all.

The year I turned 55 brought more changes. I took an exit package, and my marriage began to unravel. I gave myself a year off. I'd been working since I was 19. Now, with no kids at home, no marriage and no job, I hit a wall. If a movie title could sum up that year of my life, it would be 'It's Complicated Up In The Air.'

I went into therapy and began training for a three-day breast cancer fundraising walk that one of my best friends had long wanted me to do but I was always too busy working. The group of women I trained with became an important part of my life.

All of the soul searching made me realize I could seize my life –or drown. I told myself, 'This is who I am, and I can't live with a fake version any longer.'

I was recruited to this new role as CEO of Artful Home, an online company that sells artist-made decor and jewelry, and I'm the happiest I've ever been. I've come full circle—it brings together my training as an artist and my experience in retail. And I feel like I'm just hitting my stride."

Last week, you created a profile of your professional self. In doing so, you filled in the first variable of the Ripe equation: [experience + passion = ripening]. You know what you do well, what you have to offer, what your capacity is. Now, you need to start thinking about the second Ripe factor—what will make you want to leap out of bed, eager to work?

This week and next, you're going to do what Lisa Bayne did for herself—go behind the scenes and get to know yourself better. You'll create a truly personal profile by uncovering the "you" that lies beneath that polished exterior everyone knows, which has served you so well.

Why do we need to do this? Because the ripening journey is also a voyage of self discovery. Our work will only be "rich and rewarding" if we know what makes us happy, what our values are, and what we need now.

This may be the first time you're questioning yourself in this way. It's not surprising. We've all been busy building careers and providing for our families. Plus, contemplation is not a trait widely encouraged in our society—we're focused on doing rather than reflecting. Consider Twitter. The question 175 million "Tweeters" answer each day is not "How are you feeling?," but "What's happening?"

And your values may not have been rewarded before now— you may have been required to take on those of your profession or employer. However, your values matter a great deal. In fact, being clear about what's important to you is essential to your ripening.

At this stage of our lives, many of us feel compelled to stop and assess. Of course, events happen that force us to do this as well—job loss, divorce, illness. Our parents die. Our friends do, too. And we have a growing sense of our own mortality. All those things that, aside from maturity, give us perspective (or a reality check).

As Lisa Bayne discovered during her transitional year ("It's Complicated Up In The Air"), as unpleasant as it is, upheaval gives us a chance to discover what's most important in life, and to reconnect with our true selves. Rod Schwartz is another good example. Rod, 54, is a social venture capitalist and a colleague I run in to from time to time. One evening, as we were leaving a conference, he told me he was recently divorced, and living on his own—something he had never done before. "You're getting to know yourself again," I said. He nodded. "For the first time, Julia, for the first time."

We're not imagining our midlife ennui. Something deep and universal happens at this age. Research shows at 50 we are at our lowest ebb and less happy than at any other stage of life, even when all the usual suspects—from health through income—are accounted for. (The good news: studies show it gets better from here. More to come on this, so keep reading!)

Whatever the reason—whether it's something bubbling up from deep inside or external circumstances, or both—we arrive at this point on our life journey and realize the terrain has changed, and so have we. It's time for something new. But what? And how do we find our way?

This chapter is designed to help you begin the process of inquiry that will lead to your answer. As you work through it, ask your critical self (the part of your brain that is analytical—

and, let's face it, the one that can be self-destructive, too) to take a back seat for now. The same holds true for your Ripe Kitchen Cabinet, the team of advisors you assembled in Week Two. They'll play a role—a vital role—later in the process, but you don't need them at this stage.

Why? Because, as you open up, as you move closer to your essential self, you may feel tender and sensitive, or even disoriented and uncertain. What you need most of all is the loving, unconditional support of your Ripe Circle. They'll help you keep your mind and heart open to whatever comes.

Who Am I?

Last week, you wrote the story of your working life. Now, we'll add personal details to this work in progress, recording the major events in your life, people you've met, places you've been.

Sometimes when I propose this to my clients, I see them sag a little. "Oh, no, another thing for my to-do list," one woman mumbled. Others protest more directly, "I already know my life story!" And, of course you do. But, just as you've already discovered with your career story, putting things down on paper helps you see yourself in a new way, and gain insight into what might lie ahead.

Many Ripe pioneers gained insight by taking time off, sometimes as long as a year. In therapy, on their own or on long walks with friends, they pored over the details of their lives, searching for connections and meaning, and for clues about the path forward. Media executive Barbara Johnson (who we meet later in Week Eight), made several important realizations when she took time off to think about her future, "I knew I had too much energy not to work. But it was also clear that I needed to do something different. I didn't want it to be about money, period."

As you write, take time to cherish yourself, savour your successes, mourn your losses, and really acknowledge the milestones. My informed guess is that, no matter how you're feeling about your life when you begin this exercise, you'll end up thinking, "Wow, what a ride!"

What Do I Want?

Kevin Jones, a successful entrepreneur, was poised to launch a new business. Standing in the kitchen one day, chatting with his 21-year-old daughter, she suddenly turned to him and asked, "Dad, what's the meaning of your life?"

Kevin told me the question set him back on his heels. "As a child of the '60s, I was astonished to discover I didn't have an answer. And I wanted one that satisfied both of us."

He realized in his 50s he didn't just want to make money—not that it isn't satifying, but it was no longer enough. He wanted something more meaningful—as his daughter helped him recognize in the way only those who know and love us can.

Kevin's story reminded me that as we ripen, we are doing what young people do. They are in the process of becoming—and so are we. Who are we now and what do we want from our work? What were the things we thought we'd do when we were younger? And do we want to pick up where we left off?

Many of us have spent our lives doing for others. For decades, we have been responsible citizens, doing what we thought was right. Rosa Lee Harden, who has been an entrepreneur and a parish priest, as well as a mother and wife (of Kevin Jones above), put it this way, "When I was young, I believed you went to college, got married, settled down and went about your life, including paying off your mortgage and contributing to your retirement savings."

It's not uncommon for women to feel pulled between duty and desire—many of us spend our adult lives caring for others. Whether full-time or not, being a mother is all-consuming. "Children take up 50 percent of your cranium," former advertising exec Betty Londergan told me. "You don't really know that until it's over." Many of the women I interviewed spoke about how, as much as they loved being a mother, they were glad when that phase of parenting was behind them. The most common refrain? "It's my turn now."

Jacqueline Kennedy Onassis is a particularly poignant example. She grew up in an era when women were expected to play supporting roles, something she did very well—as First Lady and then as a kind of "first mother" to a nation in mourning. At midlife, she broke the mold by going into publishing, a career that put her lifelong passion for reading—combined with her considerable intellect—to work. (Thinking about Washington wives, I find myself wondering how Michelle Obama will ripen, or Tipper Gore.)

Not to say there aren't plenty of men who feel it's their turn now, too, as one of my male readers reminded me when I shared early drafts of *Ripe*. When I saw his comment in the margins, it took me back to the day when my father announced that he would never, ever wear a tie again. He had been a dutiful provider, but those days were now officially behind him. Interestingly, my younger brother Jeff is now in the same boat, having broken free of the golden handcuffs of corporate life in his late 40s in order to work for himself.

To help you switch gears from being duty-minded to desire-driven, instead of a "to-do" list, I want you to think about a "what-do-I-want-to-do?" list. What's important to you now? What can you give yourself permission to wonder about, to explore? You may realize you're capable of more than you ever dreamed. Editor Andrea Knight summed-up perfectly how many of us are feeling: "At 57, I feel in control of my life for the first time. I want to keep moving through my fear and resistance to try new things, because I want to do it all. And I don't want to have any regrets."

What Would Ripe Work Look Like?

Now that we have knowledge, skills and resources—and a growing sense of what we want in the years to come—let's start to imagine what our Ripe role might look like.

What kind of work do you want to do now? Can you see yourself continuing on your current path, but with renewed passion for your career? Or do you want to try something new?

As you imagine your ripening, don't worry about the details just yet—never mind title, profession, sector. Stay with generalities. How hard you want to work may be something to consider, as it was for social innovator David Simms. "For me, the treadmill went from fast to faster," he said. Asking yourself what would make you want to get out of bed each day is also helpful. Here's how writer Rona Maynard described what she was looking for: "The bottom line is I want to get up in the morning eager to think about my work. It has to be something where I can use my love of problem-solving, because I enjoy cracking my head. Whatever I do next has to be big and unwieldy and thorny with lots of mysteries."

Is it important, for instance, to bring your authentic self to work—to be your full, real self in your new role? Many Ripe pioneers told me acting the way others wanted them to now took too much energy. Barbara Johnson put it this way, "At this age, we're not interested in pretending anymore." I remember hearing Oprah Winfrey talk about how the closer she got to being her real self on air, the more she connected with her audience (and the better her ratings fared). It's true for me, too. I've discovered the more authentic I am when giving a speech, the more things flow. I measure this partly by the energy in the room, and partly by how many hands go up at the end.

• • •

Reflection is the pause that refreshes. It gives us a chance to step off the fast track and consider ourselves from a fresh perspective.

In Week Five we're going to dig even deeper. I know from experience some people aren't interested in further inner exploration. But if you are brave enough to push beyond your comfort zone and even a little curious about what might lie ahead, then stay with us. Even greater resources lie deep inside that will enrich this process and the end result. As you know, reward doesn't come without risk—the next chapter will benefit your soul as well as your search.

Journal

• Who am I?
Add to your life story, this time focusing on personal details. Do it the same way you did your work history. You might consider buying a huge roll of paper, pinning it up on the wall or stretching it out across the floor, and using coloured pens to highlight the major events, key people and places that stand out.

• What do I want?
Imagine the interview we began last week ("give me a quick sketch of your career") is continuing. Tell me what you're looking for in the next phase of your life. What's important to you now? What do you want to do? And what do you never want to do again? One of my clients, a recent refugee from the corporate world, memorably said the first time we met, "I never want to see my name on another 'org chart' as long as I live!"

• What would Ripe work look like?
Let's continue the interview. Jot down what comes to you as you read through this section. Really visualize yourself in the role—where are you? How do you spend your days?

Think about people, too. What are they like? How do you work with them? Are you leading? On a team? Consider place as well. Are you at home? In an office tower? An ivory one? On a farm? A beach? A ship?

Is it important to you to be authentic? Who is the real you? What does writing your life story help you see that you hadn't noticed before? Remember, you don't have to think about details such as profession, title and organization just yet. Stay with generalities for now.

Be careful who you share your vision with—not everyone sees the world the way you do. Not everyone is eager to see you ripen. Look for caring, compassionate, positive, supportive people when you begin to go public. Your Ripe Circle is your best bet (the Kitchen Cabinet folks can come on board later!).

Spadework

1. Ripe Credo. Now that you're connecting with your authentic self, try writing a phrase that describes who you are and how you want to live and work now. It can be a few words or a few sentences. For instance, mine is "positive, constructive, hopeful."

2. Refer back to your Ripe Principles that you created in Week Two to help guide your journey. Do you need to add anything or change them in any way?

3. Let's check again to see whether anything impedes your ripening. Objections from loved ones (or from yourself)? How might you respond in a way that acknowledges what's going on, and allows you to move forward? For instance, "I understand that this is new and scary for both of us. It's also something I really want to try. Can you trust me and give me the time and space I need to do my best?"

4. Who would you like to work with? Why? Think about people you know, those you've met, and those you've heard about. Jane Goodall and Judi Dench would be on my list.

5. If you could do anything, what would it be?

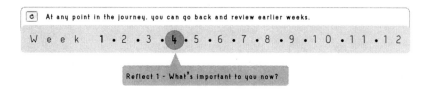

At any point in the journey, you can go back and review earlier weeks.

Week   1 • 2 • 3 • 4 • 5 • 6 • 7 • 8 • 9 • 1 0 • 1 1 • 1 2

Reflect 1 - What's important to you now?

Week Four in Review

- Now, you're filling in the second variable: [experience + passion = ripening].

- To discover your new passion, you need to get to know yourself better (perhaps for the first time).

- Reflection is the pause that refreshes. It's a chance to step off the fast track and consider ourselves from a fresh perspective.

- Tell your life story, savouring successes, mourning losses and celebrating milestones.

- Forget the "to-do" list. Create a "what-do-I-want-to-do?" list.

- Ask yourself what's important to you now. What would stretch you in new directions?

- What kind of work do you want to do? Stay with generalities for now.

- Who is the authentic you?

WEEK FIVE:
Reflect II

"Real discovery lies outside the ring of existing knowledge."
- Samuel Chao Chong Ting

What's on the horizon?
Connect with a deeper sense of who you are.

Lee Weinstein, 51, from corporate executive to entrepreneur

"I grew up thinking I'd run for office and change the world somehow. My first real job was working for Oregon's member of Congress in D.C.. After that, I did a stint for the governor of this state, worked for an AIDS agency and then returned to Oregon to join Nike, working in public relations and communications.

One morning, as I was getting ready to go to work, I realized my 15-year anniversary with the company was approaching. I looked in the bathroom mirror and asked myself if I wanted to be there for another 15. And the guy in the mirror came back with an expletive and a vehement 'No!'

At that point I realized, 'God, I've got to make a change.'

And that thought scared the heck out of me. I had a six-figure salary with stock options and great benefits—not to mention wonderful people to work with. But I really didn't want to do it any more.

The thing that was even more shocking was I had no idea what I did want to do. I'm goal-oriented, so not having one was frightening.

I started looking around, wondering what other jobs I might do, thought about talents I thought I had, and did some soul searching. A career counsellor suggested I write an autobiography –to think about who I was and where I came from. That was helpful. She also said I needed to deconstruct because I'd been on the Autobahn going 180 m.p.h. for decades. I had to go off-road and stimulate my brain in a different way. She recommended going into the wilderness.

I found being in nature incredibly useful. Some of my greatest epiphanies came while sitting next to the Salmon River in Oregon, like the idea that my wife and I needed to do what we'd been talking about for years—move to the country.

I did some more thinking on my own, and then went to work with a therapist I knew. She didn't specialize in careers, but agreed to help me reflect, to think about what I might do.

I started coming up with career options, like buying a local pizza franchise and opening it somewhere in the countryside. And then I hit on the idea of doing free-writes every morning. Come up with different scenarios. I made up some rules that I would write as long as I could without stopping, that I wouldn't correct spelling, delete or change anything. I wrote about becoming director of a museum, working at a large, international PR firm, taking a job as an English teacher.

One morning I wrote, 'It's 6 a.m. and I'm waking up in the Columbia Gorge and I've got my own business ...' I got such a charge, I just knew that was it. I was so excited and certain, I called my mother right away and said, 'I'm moving out to the gorge and starting my own company!' I still had no idea it was going to be a PR firm, or that Nike would be one of my first clients, but I knew I was on my way."

Though it was a shock to realize one path had ended, and incredibly difficult to find his way, Lee Weinstein not only persevered, he triumphed. And so will you.

Of course, I understand it may not feel that way at the moment. Not long ago, one of my clients sat before me and wept. She insisted, at 55, the best of life was behind her. "It's over," she sobbed. I listened with deep empathy, knowing that many people feel the same way. And then I told her about Doris McCarthy.

Doris McCarthy bloomed late. Though she had painted since her youth, it wasn't until her retirement from teaching at the age of 62 that she took up her life's work. But first she had to overcome some powerful social conditioning. "When I retired from teaching I thought the next major event of my life would be dying," she told me. "There was no imagining that the best years were still ahead of me." Doris became one of Canada's most renowned artists, with works in public and private collections around the world. She was still painting when she died, at 100, in November 2010.

By now, we know our working lives aren't over. But we're still searching for the answer to the central question, "What's next?" And though it's tempting to make a quick decision, if we rest a little longer in the uncertainty, our answer will be more original—and more rewarding. That's something researchers know very well. The quote that opens this chapter, "real discovery lies outside the ring of existing knowledge" comes not from an ancient Chinese philosopher but from MIT professor and Nobel laureate Samuel Chao Chung Ting. At 74, he and his team of scientists are exploring the mysteries of "dark matter" in space.

This week, we're going to do a little exploration of our own. Self-exploration. As we do, I encourage you to go as far and as fast as feels right, choosing the exercises and answering the questions that call to you. As you've discovered, all kinds of thoughts and feelings can be aroused by this journey. And this week can be especially intense, particularly if you're not given to reflection or don't already have a contemplative practice that connects you to your deeper self—such as prayer, meditation or psychotherapy.

Keep your Ripe Circle—your support group—close by for kind and loving attention. Do this week's work in a private, safe and comfortable place. (If you haven't already set up this space for yourself, or a Ripe Circle, please do so now.) And if this part of your ripening journey ever becomes too emotionally difficult, feel free to stop. I'm a big proponent of professional support for the deepest parts of our journey toward self-knowledge, so if you're feeling exceptionally unsettled, curious to know more, or simply want someone to talk to, please reach out to a spiritual leader, a psychotherapist or a coach. Lee Weinstein did, as he mentioned in his story at the start of this chapter. And so did many other Ripe pioneers, including educator Murray Kelley: "I went back into therapy to talk about what this next phase might be. Doing weekly reflection with my therapist is one of my strategies for exploring what might be and being present to what is going on inside of me."

Childhood

The first time I heard about the acorn theory—the notion that everything the mighty oak will become is contained in that one tiny seed—I was fascinated. It's a rich metaphor for what happens when we ripen. What did your acorn contain and how will it continue to unfold?

I asked consultant John Elkington (who we meet later in Week Nine) about his childhood. "I read voraciously as a child. If someone had told me at the age of 11 that I would eventually write several books, I wouldn't have believed them. If they'd said one day I'd speak at 500 major conferences around the world, I would absolutely not have believed them because I was catatonically shy. Yet, it was in me, waiting to emerge." As he was sharing this insight, I thought of author Graham Greene's line, "There is always one moment in childhood when the door opens and lets the future in."

In Week Four, when you were writing your autobiography,

did you include your childhood? These years contain many clues that can help guide our future. What were you like as a child? What did you love to do? What were you discouraged from doing? What do you still hold dear—or long to pick up again? What have you lost? Think about what you truly love, your talents, your traits.

As we've already seen, the pursuit of authenticity is a critical part of the ripening journey. What does the child inside have to tell us about who we really are? And who we want to be now?

Deeper

Once you've looked at your past, you can take a deeper look at the present. One of the great joys of reaching this age is realizing we're no longer interested in just the surface of life—we now want the pearls at the bottom of the sea. And we know the only way to get to them is to dive deep.

Although we know this is true, sometimes when I'm leading a Ripe workshop and the slide "deeper" appears on the screen, I see people shift uncomfortably in their seats. Sensing this, I move quickly to an explanation of what I mean, much as I did at the beginning of this chapter—we're simply going to engage the part of our mind that is usually beyond our awareness.

Psychology calls this the subconscious. My clients describe it in a range of ways—everything from soul to spirit to God to "the universe." I prefer the term psyche, so that's what I'll use. But feel free to use a word that feels right to you.

The psyche is always with us—even if we're not aware of it. Our real work is to establish a connection with it so we can hear what it has to say.

Lynn Mizono understands this concept very well. A

successful clothing designer, she sensed, after 27 years in business, it was time for a change. Searching for an answer, she moved to Whidbey Island near Seattle. She continued to run her business, commuting from there to California.

Then, one day, some deep, knowing part of her made it perfectly clear it was time to stop. "I got a really bad case of sciatica," she told me. "It was so bad I couldn't leave the house for six months." And that turned out to be a gift. "The fact that I couldn't do anything kept me in the place of being." New ideas emerged from this period of reflection: Lynn sold her business and became an artist.

So, how do we connect? As Ripe pioneers discovered, anything that takes us off the fast track, moves us from an external to internal focus, and brings us into our bodies as well as the present moment can work. Physical things can do this—such as gardening, running, yoga or dancing. For some, nature does the trick. Routine can do it, too—washing dishes, vacuuming, brushing the dog. Non-verbal communication is another option, including music or art, or something actively contemplative (if that's not an oxymoron), such as prayer and meditation. Finally, reverie is a tried-and-true method of artists —lots of them stare off into space as they're waiting for their character to speak or the way forward to appear. The way artist and film-maker Julian Schnabel, 60, described his artistic process sounds right for ripening, too. "I don't know what it's going to look like when I'm done, but I know how to start, how to lean toward the divine light. I figure it out as I go along, and in the process of doing, the thing emerges."

However you connect, you're sending a clear signal to your psyche: in the immortal words of TV's Dr. Frasier Crane, "I'm listening!" When you establish this vital link, your psyche will deliver. Guaranteed. Your inner GPS will communicate with you—offering up insights, ideas and inspiration.

You'll also need to become adept at noticing what drifts into your conscious awareness—and then figuring out how to decode those clues. That's right, your psyche doesn't speak in plain language. As you've no doubt noticed whenever you recall your dreams, your inner adventurer prefers symbols and metaphor. Recently, I did a big clean-out at home, getting rid of years of collected stuff. In one closet I found a painting I'd made nearly 10 years ago, and had forgotten about: three bananas stacked on top of one another, in various stages of ripening. I called it "banana yesterday, banana today, banana tomorrow." Looking at it again, I started to laugh. Clearly, I had painted what was going on inside of me at the time—as I began my own midlife journey. Even better, my psyche gave me the title for the book I would someday write—"*Ripe*."

Emerging

Things surface at this stage of life that would never have been possible in our youth.

Ripe pioneers talk about feeling different after 50. Counsellor Bob Keteyian spoke about feeling more at ease, more self-assured: "I'm sitting in my own skin better. I have a quiet confidence now." Social innovator Marilyn Strong found her focus had shifted. "There's something about turning 50 where you stand in your own power and care less about what others want you to be."

Research tells us new qualities emerge at midlife—and later. Older people are better able to see the big picture, more likely to come up with solutions to conflict, and (here's one employers will love!) more likely to show up for work. The people I interviewed for this book agree. Lawyer Alan Spinrad told me, "I'm more focused on intention than outcome. And

I'm more patient—years of experience have taught me that every deal, every case, has its own process." Social innovator David Simms talked about how he's more willing to listen to others: "Earlier in my career, I didn't get the importance of people. When you realize there is so much wisdom in others, you get to a better place. I've gotten better at involving others." And human-resources professional Kelly McDougald could see how the challenges she's faced have honed her. "I'm more resilient, for sure. And I understand the grey zone better, too," she said. "I'm less idealistic in terms of thinking that things have to be black and white."

The value of older people is beginning to be recognized—and in surprising ways. In Silicon Valley, for example, bringing in a business veteran to help with a start-up is known as "adult supervision." Perhaps the most powerful example of this shift comes from recent events in Chile, where mining foreman Luis Urzua, 54, emerged as an inspirational leader. His presence of mind kept 33 men alive and sane while they were trapped underground, until they could be rescued two months later.

• • •

Have you reread your first journal entries lately? If you do, you'll notice your thinking and awareness are changing. You know yourself better now, and have a growing sense of where you're going.

After a period of retreat, it's time to advance. In Week Six, we'll venture beyond ourselves.

Journal

• Childhood

Close your eyes to your current world and responsibilities. Imagine you are in your childhood home, garden, or with a special friend. What do you see? What did you like to do? What do you like about yourself—what traits or qualities do you remember with pleasure? Which ones surprise you? What do you miss?

If you can't remember much about your childhood—which some of us can't—is there someone in your life who might help? A friend who was there, who can help recreate your childhood with great care and attention.

• Deeper

As I write, it's Winter Solstice in the Northern Hemisphere. I think about how many cultures have rituals to celebrate the "coming of the light" (with Christmas being just one example). What can you do that might signal to your psyche that you, too, are looking for the light? For insight?

Robert Louis Stevenson, author of *Treasure Island*, *Strange Case of Dr. Jekyll and Mr. Hyde* among others, acknowledged that much of his work came to him in his dreams. The trick, he said, was asking for input before he fell asleep. Here's how he described his night-time muse: "My Brownies, who do one-half of my work for me while I'm asleep, and in all human likelihood, do the rest for me as well, when I am wide awake and fondly suppose I do it for myself."

Take time this week to establish a connection with your inner adventurer or muse. Choose one way or try a few and see what's best for you. Notice what comes out of the blue. Reflect on what it means to you, and how it might influence your ripening. Share it with your Ripe Circle, too.

Once you've connected with your inner GPS, make sure to check back in with your younger self. Are you better able to connect with the child inside of you, and remember more about those years?

• Emerging

What are you capable of at midlife that you weren't before? What words would you use to describe yourself—qualities, traits—that wouldn't have applied when you were younger? How might these add to your sense of mastery? To your pursuit of a new passion? Thinking back to Week Three, can you add to your list of strengths?

Spadework

1. Feeling the impulse to de-clutter? Great! Getting rid of the old prepares us to welcome the new. This includes stuff, bad habits and toxic friendships. Just let it go so the new you has room to flourish.

2. What's your wildest dream? I pinged a bunch of people when I was writing this section of the book and got some thrilling responses. One friend replied immediately, "I want to be a singer!" (I laughed out loud— me, too! We're the generation who dreamed of ending up on the cover of *Rolling Stone*. Considering the huge success of the video game, "Guitar Hero," this dream hasn't gone away.) Write down your wildest dream. Then, say it out loud. Yes, you can!

    Go ahead, do it. Another response to my email query was, "I want to draw cartoons!" Take a risk: do a little of whatever your dream might be. Send that cartoon to the local paper, start a blog, or enter a caption in the *New Yorker*'s weekly cartoon contest.

3. Body talk. Let your physical self show you the way. Do something that will get you out of your head and into your body. What appeals to you? Dancing? Drumming? Chanting? Or get down on the floor and pretend you're a young child again. Make shapes with your body, crawl, lie on your back and wave your legs and arms in the air. It may feel silly at first—or it might feel splendid. But try it, and see what comes. (And welcome whatever it might be—even if it's a fit of laughter.)

4. Om. Everybody's tried some kind of contemplative practice by now, right? We've all done yoga or meditation or prayer. Give yourself some time to leave the world behind and go inside—and make sure to put up a do-not-disturb sign, virtual or otherwise. Burn incense, light a candle, put on some Gregorian chants or, if you prefer, gospel or classical music. And then just be with what comes. Keep your journal handy.

5. Draw. Let's engage your inner adventurer in a different way. Draw a picture of yourself in a boat. No other instructions. Just have fun with it (use crayons or coloured markers!). Draw whatever comes. (And if your inner critic really, really doesn't want you to draw because—oh, I don't know, it thinks you're lousy at it—do it anyway. No one has to see what you create but you.)

6. Are you getting the support you need from your Ripe Circle? Do you need to add or subtract people?

↺ At any point in the journey, you can go back and review earlier weeks.

W e e k   1 • 2 • 3 • 4 • **5** • 6 • 7 • 8 • 9 • 1 0 • 1 1 • 1 2

Reflect II – Dive deep to discover pearls of insight.

Week Five in Review

- It's important to journey deeper into ourselves to find our new passion.

- If we can rest in the uncertainty a little longer, our answer will be more original—and more rewarding.

- What were you like as a child? What did you love? What have you lost?

- Find ways to connect with your psyche, with your inner GPS. Then, pay attention to what comes and learn to decipher it.

- What's emerging in you at this age that wasn't there before—what kinds of qualities or traits?

WEEK SIX:
Reconnoiter

"I have greatly enjoyed the second blooming. Suddenly you find—at the age of 50—that a whole new life has opened before you."
- Agatha Christie

What's on the horizon?
Experiment and observe the world around you.

Andrea Knight, 57, from freelance editor to fulfilled editor

"I was a high school dropout. It was the '60s, and I went to live on Canada's east coast for five years. While there, I started taking adult-ed courses and discovered my passion for learning. I helped found the first women's centre in Fredericton, New Brunswick, the first women's crisis centre, and sat on the board of the women's newspaper.

When I returned to Toronto, I went back to school and got half way through my PhD before I dropped out again, this time to work for Dr. Henry Morgentaler. I was executive director of his abortion clinic for five years.

After that, I was a freelance editor for 15 years, many of them with publisher Malcolm Lester. I edited a number of Holocaust survivor memoirs, and learned more about my own family's history. I kept thinking someone should be collecting all of these stories so they don't get lost.

In my mid-50s, I was ready for another change. My marriage had ended and I was a single parent with two teenaged daughters. The freelance life is hard and, so, for stability and sanity, I decided it was time to look for full-time work.

One evening, I went to a book launch. Chatting with some people I knew, I mentioned I was looking for a full-time gig and did anyone know of anything? No one did. But a week later, a book designer called and said he'd heard about an opportunity and immediately thought of me.

As soon as he told me what it was—editing a series of Holocaust memoirs—I thought, 'That's my job!' The feeling I was meant for this work gave me the confidence to go after it.

I called immediately and discovered they were launching the first series of memoirs the very next day! My spirit soared. The *event was fully booked, but I wouldn't take no for an answer. I explained who I was and why I wanted to come. And they put me on the list.*

The evening was wonderful, and I made a point of finding Naomi Azreili, then executive director and now chair and president of the foundation. She said, 'We need to talk.'

A week later, we met. And two weeks after that, I got the job."

How did Andrea Knight find her brilliant new career? She got up off the couch and went outside. And that's precisely what we need to do now.

Midway through our ripening journey, it's time to reconnoiter—throw open the doors and look at the world around us. To expand our horizon. To see what appeals and where the opportunities are.

This week, you'll be looking for the thing that makes you feel alive and engaged, the idea or enterprise that gives you new energy. To paraphrase Graham Greene, it's about discovering which new door will open and let the rest of your future in.

It's impossible to know where this exploration will lead us or how far we have to go. Our reconnoitering might take us to the other side of the planet or we may discover what we're looking for is very close, indeed.

Not long ago, on my way to give a speech, I was walking across a university campus and fell in step with someone who was headed the same way. I asked him for directions to a particular hall. We exchanged pleasantries about the weather, then—without sharing what I do or mentioning this book—I asked him what he did for a living. "I've been working for this university for nearly 30 years. Recently, I tried a completely new job—that's what midlife is all about, right, reinvention? I thought that's what I needed. I soon realized I was miserable, totally miserable. I couldn't go back to my old job and had no idea what to do. Eventually, I found a new one doing the same kind of work. And that made all the difference. It's familiar, but the people are new. Turns out, that's all I needed. Even just a different route to work, seeing a different part of the campus after all these years helps. I feel refreshed, like I've got wind under my wings." And, with that, he dashed into a building, waving goodbye. I smiled. He thought he had to go somewhere dramatically different but, for him, a small change was all it took.

Look, Listen

This week is about feeding yourself—filling up on new ideas and different points of view. The goal here is to open your mind to new possibilities.

And one of the best ways to do this is to tune into the millions of conversations taking place across our planet all day, every day, in the media and on the Internet. Start by looking for new areas of interest and topics that appeal—anything and everything. Be an omnivore. Devour political stories and documentaries about ring-tailed lemurs, articles about wind power and think pieces on finance. By all means, if you have a keen interest or nascent passion, follow that impulse. But don't close the door to the wider world just yet. Really stretch beyond what you would normally peruse.

Then, let your tastes and sources narrow naturally over time. Start to follow the writers, film-makers and journalists you admire. They'll be a constant source of inspiration and information—and may even do some of your spadework for you. Blogger Betty Londergan is a great example. "I'm learning so much, talking to all of these really incredible people, learning about all of the possibilities that are out there for me—for all of us."

When you feel ready, move beyond listening, reading and observing, and join the conversation by contributing your own thoughts. And choose your conversations with care. Avoid what long-time *New York Times* columnist William Safire memorably called the "nattering nabobs of negativity." You're looking for positive, constructive, hopeful people. Select sources and voices whose outlook on life is aligned with your Ripe Credo.

As you do all of this, pay attention to what's going on around you in your daily life. The chance encounters. The things that drift into your consciousness. The very thing you're looking for might just be there. As Ripe pioneer Val Fox says, "Life throws things your way, and it's up to you to notice. You've got to pick up on it."

Social innovator Barbara Johnson certainly found this to be true. "I came out of my year of reflection and started talking to everyone I know, including my sister who lives in Madison, Wisconsin. Out of the blue, she said, 'You know, next time you're out here, you really should meet Pleasant Rowland, the woman who started the American Girl company. I think you two would really get along.' So, the next time I was in Madison, I made a point of meeting Pleasant. And the rest is history!" (You'll read more about Barbara's ripening from media executive to director of a reading program for kids in Week Eight.)

Call it luck, coincidence or synchronicity, my ripening has been filled with these kinds of memorable experiences, too. In the summer of 2010, I was assembling a team of interns to work with me on this book. Lots of people applied. One young woman I interviewed mentioned she'd read my first book. Thinking she meant *We Are The New Radicals*, which had recently been published, I murmured "thank you" and moved on. "*Green is Gold*," she said emphatically. Oh. That was the title of my first book—one of the first environmental primers for business—published 20 years earlier when she would have been, I guessed, about five. How had she heard about it? "My high school teacher recommended it to me." Interesting. Where did she go to high school? "Dubai." As that sunk in, she went on. "Oh, Julia, you have no idea how important your words were to me. I felt like a crazy person in a land that only exists to make money." Two decades later, and half a world away, she'd found my name on a website and reached out, hoping to work with me.

Coincidence? I think not! My point is, call them what you like, these things happen to all of us. Watch for them to see if something pops up you want to pursue.

Explore, Connect

Young people learn about themselves by going places, meeting people and trying new things. Now it's our turn to do this all over again—to explore the world and see what makes us feel energized and inspired.

As you do this week's "Look, Listen" research, you'll come across all kinds of interesting events and conferences. Go to as many of them as you can manage not only to learn what others are doing, but also to see who you meet.

If resources are a challenge, be creative. Social media consultant Debbie Dimoff was. "As I was trying to figure out my next incarnation, I wanted to find out everything that was going on. But thinking about the price tag to do it all made me queasy. I decided to call up the organizers of the events at the top of my list, tell them I needed a complimentary pass, and offer my services in exchange—I'd facilitate a session, for instance. And everyone said yes."

Taking a course—just for interest's sake with no strings attached—can also open up the horizon. Entrepreneur Laurie Orlov discovered this for herself. "My mother died of Alzheimer's disease in 2006, which was a consciousness-raising experience for me. I became incredibly interested in elder care, not because I was thinking of it as a future career, but simply because I wanted to learn all about it. In the end, it did become my new work, but it began as a deeply personal interest."

As you explore, you're building your ripening network. New people will come into your life. Some may lead you to work, some may become part of your Ripe Circle or Ripe Kitchen Cabinet. Others may become friends. Barbara Johnson, the former media executive who became a social innovator put it this way, "What happens is we change our circle, and not even consciously. I had worked in midtown Manhattan for 20 years, commuting to jobs in law, finance and media. When I took a year off to think about my future, I went to events in my community and started meeting new people. They were the ones who supported my changing priorities."

Practise, Practise

What's the best way to see if something fits? Try it on for size. I often urge my clients to volunteer, intern or job shadow. We also talk about identifying people who are doing work that fascinates them—and offering to buy them a cup of coffee (it never hurts to ask!).

We're looking for information that will help us think clearly about our ripening. For instance, what does it take to become an entrepreneur? What capabilities are required? How do people fund their new ventures? Or, what's involved in being an artist? Where do their ideas come from? And how do they keep going when working without deadlines, in isolation, and with little or no income?

Marilyn Strong, who offers alternative funeral services and calls herself a "death midwife" took this approach: "I'm a funeral director apprentice. I wanted to get some experience in this business, to learn more about it. That way, I can decide if I want to get my licence and introduce new ideas into an established profession or continue developing my service, independent of the mainstream."

Marilyn is such a brave soul. Even when she felt doubt and anxiety about her new profession, she steadfastly pursued her groundbreaking new work. And her example brings up an important point. As we move beyond thinking and dreaming into action, fear can raise its head. People often tell me they're worried they'll make a fool of themselves. Or fail. I tell them it's OK—and natural—to feel this way, but not to let it immobilize them.

Many successful people have sat before me in the same state. Robert Pardo was a business professor at a leading North American university. At 52, after two decades of teaching, he was bored. He wanted to feel passionate about his work again but didn't know how. And some powerful impediments stood in his way. One, he was financially secure and he had tenure, so his job was secure, too. Two, he was terrified of trying something new. As we worked together, he began to see that he could continue to learn and grow, and taking risks was good for him.

Soon, he was able to articulate what he really wanted: to become a better teacher, a great teacher. With professional support (the university where he worked had just started offering coaching for its teachers), he did just that. Robert is now winning teaching awards and actively mentoring younger professors.

• • •

"If you put a bunch of mice in a box and do an MRI scan, you'll see just a few neurons developing," explains Veronika Litinski, project leader of Cogniciti, a Canadian company that develops products, games and training procedures based on brain research. "But if you put them in a space where they can swim and jump and find their way through mazes, you'll see many new neurons developing because they are being challenged."

Just like Litinski's mice, we also perform better at every level if we're stimulated. That's what reconnoitering is all about —pushing ourselves to see the world in a new way, to try the unfamiliar and discover how much we are capable of. Sparks are struck, connections made and new avenues suggested.

This week is an important milestone on your journey. You are halfway to your destination. In Week Seven we spend time getting to know some Ripe pioneers—"Masters," who stay on the same career path. Later, in Week Eight, we meet "Pathfinders," who head out in a new direction. No doubt you're curious about the joys and challenges of each.

Journal

• Look, Listen

Feed your mind by filling up on new ideas and different points of view. As you peruse the media, what comes up for you? Are you discovering new sources of information and inspiration?

What happens when you boycott negative media messages and "girlcott" those that are aligned with the Ripe Credo you created in Week Four?

• Explore, Connect

This week is about going places and meeting new people. You'll sign up for events that will take you into new territory or take a course on a new subject. How do you feel about this? As you move into the world, write about what you're learning, who you meet, and whether you have invited new people to become part of your Ripe Circle or Ripe Kitchen Cabinet.

• Practise, Practise

There's no better way to see if something works for you than to try it out. How do you feel about this idea of moving beyond thinking and dreaming into action? What are you considering trying? How about something that makes you feel like a deer caught in the headlights? For me, it was public speaking. When I first started to do it, I was absolutely terrified. I kept thinking of Eleanor Roosevelt's advice: "You must do the thing you think you cannot do." (I'm so glad I persevered, because I now love giving talks —and they're an essential part of my ripening.)

As you venture out there, come back to your journal and write about your feelings and observations. You'll be glad to have this record as you begin to make the decision about your new role.

Spadework

1. Gratitude. List five people you're glad you know. List five new people you're thrilled to have added to your network.

2. Get outside. Literally. Go for a walk, a run, a bike ride. Explore another neighbourhood. Take a different route to work. Do something you haven't done in years, maybe ice skating or line dancing. Anything that will get you out of your familiar routine—and create new neurons!

3. Strike up a conversation or two. Say hello to people you wouldn't normally notice. See what happens. Louise Bourgeois, an artist who thrived in her later years, said this was part of the secret of her success. "It's the people on the periphery who can give your life a completely different direction. It could be a conversation with a taxi driver or an epiphany with someone on the subway. And you may never see this person again."

4. Think back to the people you've met since beginning your journey. What would it be like to have lived their lives—or to be moving into their futures? How can you apply these insights to your own process?

5. Are you beginning to see a new Ripe Circle or a new community taking shape around you? If not, and you'd like to, what can you do to encourage it?

⟲ At any point in the journey, you can go back and review earlier weeks.

Week   1 • 2 • 3 • 4 • 5 • ⑥ • 7 • 8 • 9 • 10 • 11 • 12

Reconnoiter — Expand your horizon to see new opportunities.

Week Six in Review

- It's time to throw open the doors and look at the world around us.

- Tune into the millions of conversations taking place all over the world via the media or Internet. Look for topics and ideas that appeal. (Boycott negative voices and "girlcott" positive ones.)

- Get outside. Go to events and conferences. Meet new people.

- Try new things. Volunteer, intern, apprentice.

- Pay attention to what's going on around you. Watch for synchronicity.

- Keep challenging yourself, exploring, growing (and developing new neurons!).

WEEK SEVEN:
The Masters

"For me, the starting line is just coming into view."
- Gary Hirshberg, CE-Yo, Stonyfield Farms

What's on the horizon?
Discover the joys of travelling on the same career path.

If you think midlife career rejuvenation depends on reinvention, you're not alone. Baby Boomers who are bored or burned-out feel enormous pressure to change what they do for a living.

When I started on this book, I was thinking along the same lines. Everywhere I looked, there were high-profile examples of reinventors such as Sandra Day O'Connor, who stepped down the from U.S. Supreme Court and is now an educator and video game developer (games that help drive social change, of course). And Guy Laliberté, founder of Cirque du Soleil, who now invests his energy in water conservation issues and who also, in 2009, paid for the privilege (to the tune of $35-million U.S.) of being the first clown launched into space.

One day, I spotted something different—some of the newsmakers I was reading about were doing familiar work while stretching in new directions. For instance, each of 80-year-old Clint Eastwood's recent films is different in theme, narrative and visual style—consider "Gran Torino," "Invictus" and "Hereafter." At 77, Jane Goodall now travels 300 days a year, having realized the most effective way to save her beloved chimps is by connecting with audiences around the world. Even

Prince Charles, 62, has found new ways to define his title, becoming the patron saint of organic farming and delivering the keynote address at the 2009 U.N. Climate Change Conference in Copenhagen.

These people represent a distinct kind of Ripe pioneer—those who discover new passion for their careers and achieve a level of mastery previously unattainable. Former U.S. senator Ted Kennedy is perfect example. Here's what *The New York Times* printed when Kennedy died in 2009, at 77. "He gradually found his place and grew into a role where his own gifts worked perfectly. In late middle age, he built a truly spectacular career."

I call these Ripe pioneers "Masters."

It will be interesting to see how many of us become Masters. I suspect our numbers will far outstrip reinventors (who I call "Pathfinders"—more on them in Week Eight).

The evidence for this became clear during research for *Ripe*. As we were collecting clippings and transcripts, the pile with "Masters" taped on the wall above it grew much faster than the one labelled "Pathfinders." In the end, the ratio was 10 to one.

Ripe Masters are appearing in each field and every sector. Let's look at the three main types of Masters and discover how they made their choice—how they realized it was the right path for them and why it made sense to keep moving along it.

It Takes a Lifetime

Many careers require decades of service. Artists are a prime example. Picasso and O'Keeffe and composers Janáček, Verdi and Bernstein all made major contributions in their later years. Henri Matisse described his late-life work as a *"seconde vie."* More recently, in 2008, the BBC Orchestra held a centenary concert to mark the 100th birthday of composer Elliott Carter, who was not only still actively working at the time, but also the first and only "living" composer to receive the honour.

There are many careers, in fact, that require steady progress toward a long-term goal or, indeed, true mastery—science, crafts and running the family firm (including the royal family) among them. Consider, too, how many of the world's most prestigious honours are awarded to people older than 50 years of age, such the Nobel Prize.

Of course, sometimes the reward is simply the work itself.

Gary Hirshberg, 56, CE-Yo, Stonyfield Farms

"I'm a child of the '60s.

I studied climate change in college, and started working in an academic environment, researching renewable energy, organic agriculture and aquaculture.

Then came the Reagan era, when funding for everything I was doing got slashed. And I realized commerce was the only hope—ideas would only be useful if we could turn them into enterprises, and get people buying and selling these values.

My partner at the time had an incredible yogurt recipe, so we decided to start making and selling it in New Hampshire. We began with a basic question: Is it possible to create an enterprise where everybody wins? That was 27 years ago. Today, Stonyfield Farms is the largest organic yogurt company in the world.

We do $360 million in annual sales. We have sister companies in Canada, Ireland and France, with more coming. We support more than 180,000 acres of organic farmland and almost 2,000 family farms.

Every step of the way, we've checked ourselves against that original question. And we've proven what I call win-win-win-win-win enterprise is possible. The farmers are making money. Their soil is improving. Their animals are healthier. We produce a product that is good for human health. Our employees are well cared for. And our shareholders make lots of money.

So, when Danone, the world's largest yogurt maker, came along a few years ago and told me they wanted to buy Stonyfield Farms, I said, 'It's not for sale.'

Why? For me, the starting line is just coming into view. We set out to show sustainable business practices are not just a moral thing, but are actually profitable. These days, a big part of what I do is take this message out to the world—I've presented to the senior management teams of global firms such as Wal-Mart, GE, Google and Coke.

But Danone came back and said, 'We'd still like to buy your company.' And I reiterated, 'The problem is, I'm just getting started.'

In the end, we did strike a deal. They own 80 percent of the company, but I have majority control.

I feel an even greater urgency to do this work than I did 27 years ago. Almost every metric on the health of people and our planet has worsened since we started—there's still so much to do.

My own ripening is driven by a sense of what's possible and what I have left to achieve."

Discover New Passion

Many professions naturally lead to a type of ripening that enhances what people have already learned to do so well. Think of religious leaders, judges, architects, even television anchors—Diane Sawyer was named anchor of ABC's "World News" at

63. Politicians fit into this category, too—consider U.S. President Obama's surprise (and brilliant) pick for Secretary of State, Hillary Rodham Clinton.

Then there's Oprah Winfrey. Her move from broadcast to cable television—and from a daily talk show to an entire channel—is a transformative moment. To say the Oprah Winfrey Network (OWN) will be a stretch for this Master is an understatement. But she pronounces herself ready. "I'm prepared for the critics ... the naysayers," she said. Although she doesn't use the word (yet!), Oprah recognizes that she is ripening. "Everything I've ever done has prepared me for this moment, this launch."

And then there are the comeback kids, those who love what they do so much they return for another round. Fashion designer Jil Sander, 67, whose minimalist designs won her a worldwide following, left her namesake label under duress in 2004. Five years later, she was back in business, this time designing for the Japanese budget retailer Uniqlo. Actor Debra Winger, 56, walked away from her chosen profession 20 years ago to raise her family and recently decided it was time to return—and she's getting rave reviews for her role in HBO's "In Treatment." And Jerry Brown just became Governor of California for a second time at 72, after a 28-year hiatus.

What do all of these men and women have in common? They realized they still really love their work.

Marilyn Grist, 62, executive director, HelpAge USA

"I woke up at the age of 24. I'd graduated from college in journalism with every intention of becoming a writer.

When my husband and I moved to Georgia, I applied for a job with the local Community Action Program—CAP was

Lyndon Johnson's campaign against poverty. At first, I was grateful they wanted to hire me and were willing to pay me $6,000 a year to write.

But that job changed the course of my life. I'd never seen such poverty, and wanted to do whatever I could. I worked 40 hours a day and loved every bit of it.

That was the beginning of a long career in social justice. Always, my work was about the intersection of poverty and "blank"–I kept filling in the blank with something different.

When we moved to Atlanta, I heard about a job with CARE [an international poverty-fighting organization]. I stayed 20 years.

My last job with CARE was as senior vice president of external relations. I was in my 50s, had seen people linger too long, and wondered how I'd know it was time to leave. I decided to draw an arbitrary line in the sand and hold to it.

It was hard, really hard. But I knew I needed time to figure out who I was outside CARE.

At the beginning, I had this vague idea I would develop the other side of my brain. So I took sculpting classes and residential design courses.

Then the Indian Ocean Tsunami struck. I was sitting with my family, the day after Christmas 2004, watching news of what was happening in Indonesia, Sri Lanka and India. My family kept saying, 'Thank God you're not still at CARE or you wouldn't be here for Christmas!' And I agreed.

But as I lay in bed that night, I thought, 'I'm not grateful for this. I can't just sit around singing Christmas carols now.'

The tsunami taught me that I was trying to suppress something. My work is my work, and it's mine for a lifetime.

I knew I was never going to be happy unless I was part of the solution.

Over the next few years, as I took on a series of consulting projects, there was this growing sense in me that I wanted to do something on aging. I'd gone to Banda Aceh, Indonesia, after the tsunami. Standing on the shore with some local women, I saw this little island and asked if anyone on it had survived. They said not one life was lost. Why not? Because when the animals started running into the hills at six o'clock in the morning, the elders knew what it meant and quickly moved everyone up the one small mountain.

And then I heard about HelpAge International [which helps disadvantaged older people worldwide]. They asked me to do a feasibility study to launch HelpAge USA. I was about three sentences into it when I realized it was right for me.

I'm in the beginning stages of leading this organization. I feel like a freshman in college again, with so much to learn and do. I'm here for the long haul."

Come Into Our Own

Some Ripe pioneers come into their own after many years in pursuit of success. They may have been searching for the thing they are meant to do. They may have a passion, and struggle to find the time—or courage—to do it. Or they've been quietly working away on the margins for years, waiting for their moment in the spotlight.

As I mentioned earlier, women often move into a powerful, productive stage after 50—and there are hundreds of millions of us entering this period of life now. Some of us are moving into leadership roles. Consider, for example, the growing list of women on the global political stage: Australian Prime Minister

Julia Gillard, 50, German Chancellor Angela Merkel, 56, Brazil's President Dilma Rousseff, 63, and Iceland's Prime Minister Jóhanna Sigurðardóttir, 68.

Others are simply enjoying more clout, like Kathryn Bigelow. At 58, after a long career, she was nominated for an Academy Award in 2010 for her direction of the film "The Hurt Locker"—one of only four women to earn the distinction in Oscar history. When Bigelow won, her victory was celebrated by women (especially middle-aged women) around the world. Author Betty Londergan emailed me the morning after the Oscars. "How satisfying beyond belief it must have been for Ms Bigelow to not only be the first female director to win, but to beat her ex-husband, AND to look 1,000 percent better than his new wife. A trifecta!"

Like Bigelow, for some of us—men and women alike—our passion can be the full expression of what we've been honing for years.

Catherine Thompson, 53, composer, musician, artist

"I've never really had a regular job. I've always been an artist. But not a particularly driven one. I have a broad goal—I'm interested in what the world will be like when industrial civilization comes to an end—but I've always gone where the wind has taken me.

In my 20s, I went through a gender transition. It was a huge shift, and it took me 10 years to feel comfortable in my skin. Naturally, some of this has appeared in my work, but the most important lesson for me is, once you've changed your sex, there's not much you feel you can't do.

For 20 years or so, I've worked with choreographers and dance artists, composing music for their performances. I describe myself as a composer, vocalist, instrument maker, writer, musician and visual artist.

In the last few years, I've lived a nomadic life, moving from place to place, mostly in western Canada. And now every part of my life is coming together in a new work.

'The Sun and the Wind Project' is devoted to creating a deep connection to the world, the natural world. I'm going to make a long-distance horseback ride. My two horses and I will be travelling from south-central Saskatchewan, near Moose Jaw, down into Manitoba along the Montana border, and up through the foothills of the Rockies to Banff, Alberta. About 1,500 kilometres in total. I'm giving us five months.

I'll be sleeping rough alongside the horses, and giving talks in schools and concerts in communities along the way. I bought an iPhone so I can update my blog and post videos and photos. We'll see if it works all over the Prairies!

In Banff, I'll prepare the final show, combining music, storytelling and footage from our travels. I have this idea, but I know the ride itself will become the work. It's really about experiencing another way of being on the earth, another way of being with time."

• • •

Yoko Ono has been making provocative art for nearly 60 years. At 78, she continues to think long term, with several new exhibitions in the planning stages. And work on the project she and John Lennon started long ago, "Imagine Peace," continues. "When you're working, you find all this new energy. It's really not good to live by the clock."

It's clear now, just like Yoko Ono, we can find new passion for the work we've done throughout our lives. But what if we're eager to do something completely different? In Week Eight, we meet Ripe pioneers who've done just that—the "Pathfinders."

Journal

• Master

Does staying on the same path appeal to you? Is it possible to re-ignite your interest in the work you do now? Is there still more for you to do?

Do any of the Master paths make sense to you, whether it's pursuing a long-standing goal (as in the section "Takes a lifetime"), finding a fresh facet (as you read in "Discover new passion"), or fully expressing yourself (as others did in "Come into your own")?

Spadework

1. What have you secretly wanted to do in your line of work, but never had the time, courage or support to do?

2. Review your journal entries and the exercises you've been doing to see how this journey is changing you. Looking ahead, what do you imagine will happen in the weeks to come?

3. You're in Week Seven, past the halfway mark of your ripening journey. Congratulate yourself for staying the course! And reward yourself in some way. Take some personal time. Treat yourself with a favourite food or something new. Or send yourself an encouraging note—yes, really. I've written and mailed notes to myself (shades of Hugh Prather, author of *Notes to Myself*, a bestseller of our Boomer youth). I know they're coming, but not when, and it gives me a boost to read what I've written.

At any point in the journey, you can go back and review earlier weeks.

Week   1 • 2 • 3 • 4 • 5 • 6 • **7** • 8 • 9 • 10 • 11 • 12

The Masters — Finding new passion for the path you're already on.

Week Seven in Review

• Career rejuvenation doesn't depend on reinvention.

• We can discover new passion for a familiar path. And achieve a level of mastery previously unattainable.

• We can pursue a long-standing goal, like Gary Hirshberg of Stonyfield Farms.

• We can find a fresh facet, as anti-poverty activist Marilyn Grist did in choosing to lead HelpAge USA.

• We can fully express ourselves, such as artist Catherine Thompson is doing in her 50s.

WEEK EIGHT:
The Pathfinders

"I realized there simply wasn't much information out there on technology for seniors, and that insight became the impetus for a new career."
- Laurie Orlov, Founder,
Aging in Place Technology Watch

What's on the horizon?
Explore the possibilities of choosing a different career.

Reinvention holds enormous appeal for Baby Boomers like us. Who isn't eager to try something new? Who doesn't have a dream they'd love to bring to life? Who doesn't want to be part of an innovative or world-changing venture?

In an op-ed article for *The New York Times*, the paper's long-time, Pulizer-Prize-winning columnist William Safire announced his column was officially at an end. But he wasn't giving up on work—in fact, he advised against it. "Never retire," he wrote. Instead, he recommended doing something new. "Change your career to keep your synapses snapping." (Safire, himself, became chairman of The Dana Foundation, which supports research in neuroscience and brain disorders.)

Pathfinders are the Ripe pioneers everyone talks about— they leave what they know behind and set off on a great adventure. And there's a delicious—and growing—range of examples popping up all over the world.

There are Pathfinders whose new work clearly builds on what has come before. Like Maureen Taylor, 51, who spent 25 years covering medical issues for television news and then, in 2010, became one of the world's first physician assistants (a new position created to fit between an MD and a nurse practitioner). Or Albie Sachs, 75, the African National Congress activist and author who was named to South Africa's

Constitutional Court, and whose cases established global precedent.

Of course, the most surprising Pathfinders—those who take our breath away—are the ones who begin to do the thing they've longed for. Sometimes, the dream has endured for a lifetime. At 64, after a career in banking, Joel Orner told himself, "It's now or never." He enrolled in culinary school and, four years later, is chef at the Los Angeles Yacht Club. Sometimes, it's a more recent—but equally powerful—pursuit. After trying to get an invitation to the World Economic Forum in Davos, but receiving no reply, French businesswoman Aude Zieseniss de Thuin, 60, decided to create her own parallel event instead and established the Women's Forum for the Economy and Society in 2005.

We've all seen examples of Pathfinders whose new careers seem to come out of the blue. Scottish singing sensation Susan Boyle immediately comes to mind, but there's also Marla Ginsburg. A hugely successful television producer, with credits that include "La Femme Nikita" and "Highlander," Ginsburg discovered, at 50, no one would take her call. She has since reinvented herself as a designer and is now the creative director of a company that makes jeans for women *d'un certain age*, FDJ French Dressing. As she told *Businessweek*, "Whoever thought that getting older could be a career?"

Where did the passion that seized these Pathfinders come from? How did they discover it? And how did they make it their own? Let's meet three Ripe pioneers who blazed what I see as the most popular Pathfinder paths—entrepreneur, artist and social innovator.

Entrepreneurs

Arianna Huffington is a prime example. At 56, she launched the news and blog website *The Huffington Post*. Declaring it a new media model, it would welcome voices not normally heard in the mainstream press, or what she calls "curated news and instant intelligent opinion from an engaged community." In 2010, *Forbes* called Huffington a "force of nature" and put her on the list of "the most powerful women in media." (As this book goes to press, AOL announced it had just bought "the HuffPost" for $315-million and that Huffington will now lead the newly formed The Huffington Post Media Group, which will integrate content from both companies.)

It's no surprise entrepreneurship is on the rise. Many Baby Boomers—particularly those who've spent their entire careers inside global companies or in the civil service—want to set up shop on their own. To set their own agendas and spread their wings. To do their own thing.

The first time I gave a speech about *Ripe*, I asked the audience to guess the average age of first-time entrepreneurs. Some quick-witted soul piped up, "Fifty-plus!" And everyone laughed.

That gave me the set up I needed. Most of us actually carry around a very different image in our heads—when we think about entrepreneurs, we tend to think young, male, tech. And in this day and age, it's no wonder. (The 2010 film based on Mark Zuckerberg and his invention of Facebook, "The Social Network," dominated film awards. With good reason. It's not just a great film, it speaks to our fascination with entrepreneurs.) But the reality of how old entrepreneurs are when they launch their first ventures might surprise you—as it delighted my audience that morning. According to the Ewing Marion Kauffman Foundation, the world's largest foundation dedicated to entrepreneurship, the average age of first-time entrepreneurs is 55 to 64: "The U.S. is on the cusp of an entrepreneurial boom—not in spite of the aging population, but because of it."

Laurie Orlov, 59, from research analyst to new "age" analyst

"I had a consciousness-raising experience.

My mother died of Alzheimer's disease in 2006. I was the focal point of her care for eight years, investigating all of the options, including assisted-living facilities.

At that point, I'd spent my entire working life—30-plus years— working in the tech industry, ending with the market-research firm Forrester Research, working on e-commerce.

Through the experience with my mother, I became really interested in elder care. At first, I was just trying to learn about it. But it kept growing, bit by bit.

I wanted to know more, so I signed up for the University of Florida's geriatric care management program. One of my assignments was to prepare a bibliography on the 'technology for seniors' market. I immediately realized there wasn't much information out there, and that insight became the impetus for a new career—I could take the skills I'd acquired at Forrester, combine them with my new passion and launch my own venture. My company, Aging in Place Technology Watch, is a market research firm that tracks trends and analyses information about technologies for aging in your own home.

At first, I pitched the idea to Forrester and others in the industry. But no one bit. I was getting kind of whiny about it, 'Why don't these companies recognize they need me to cover this space for them at a nice high salary?' Then, one of my colleagues said, 'Why don't you just do it yourself?' And that was my 'aha!' moment."

Artists

P.D. James began writing detective novels in the 1950s. Rising early each day, she would write for several hours before leaving for work. Phyllis Dorothy James White spent 30 years in various departments of the British Civil Service, including the Police and Criminal Law Department of Great Britain's Home Office. As you can imagine, her insider's knowledge greatly enhanced her storytelling. In 2000, she celebrated her 80th birthday with the publication of her autobiography, *Time to be in Earnest.* Her latest novel, *The Private Patient,* was published in 2008. Now in her 90s, she is about to release a new book, and clearly continues to ripen. "I hope I don't disappoint readers: it's quite different from anything I've done before."

If you could do anything, what would you do? It's a question many of us would answer with "something creative." Baby Boomers perhaps even more so—those of us who didn't set out in life wanting to save the world wanted to be musicians, instead. In a recent interview, actor Colin Firth summed up his generation rather well. "I grew up wanting to be Jimi Hendrix or Keith Richards," he said. "Not some Conservative member of Parliament." (What will Joni Mitchell's "star-maker machinery behind the popular song" make of us now—is Susan Boyle just the first example of a wave of Ripe recording stars to come?)

Being "creative" can describe many things—dance, drama and drawing immediately come to mind. But, of course, creative art-forms encompass everything from the traditional, including crafts, pottery and boat-building, to the new, such as multi-media art. Are we about to witness an artistic revival—or become part of it ourselves?

Ellen Greene, 62, from educator to author

"When I met my second husband, Marshall Greene, I'd been through a series of unsuccessful relationships. I had two teenagers and swore I wasn't going to put them through that again.

I'm a notorious list person, so I decided to keep a list of anything Marshall said to me or my kids that was hurtful or harmful. That list would give me a way to cut my losses sooner.

It didn't quite work out that way. After four months, I realized I didn't have anything on the list. He was this warm-hearted gentleman who was wonderful to me and my children. They were crazy about him.

So, I thought of starting a new list and making it positive. Because this relationship was going to head south at some point— I was sure of that—I would have this list to get me through the bad times. It became a list of the everyday, nice-guy stuff he said and did. Like coming out to my car on a cold morning and discovering he'd warmed it up and scraped the ice off the windows.

He knew I was keeping it—I gave him a list each year in a Valentine's Day card. After a while, he started to play to it. I'd call him from another room and as he was closing his book and getting up from his chair he'd call out, 'Here I come, I'm ready, I'm psyched!'

And then he died. He'd struggled for eight years with Parkinson's and Alzheimer's. I was a widow at 59.

At his memorial service, a good friend of ours read some

entries from the list. Not many people knew about it then–just my children and his.

And the response was amazing. My brother, who works for Sports Illustrated in New York City, said I should write it up as an article. My draft got passed around, and eight days later Hallmark magazine called. 'We're all enthralled with Marsh. We love your story. Would $5,000 be OK?'

And then an agent from New York called and said, 'If you'd like to expand it into a book, I'd like to represent you.' He got five publishers interested, we had an auction and HarperCollins won. Within two weeks, he'd sold it to publishers in Italy, Germany, Japan and Taiwan.

Writing that book [Remember The Sweet Things: One List, Two Lives, and Twenty Years of Marriage, HarperCollins] helped me mourn and clarify issues I'd been tied up in emotional knots over. It's a sweet little love story, and I have no illusions of literary greatness. But I was a first-time author at 60, and now I'm determined to carry on. In fact, HarperCollins has an option on my second book.

I go to a lot of writing workshops. I'm blogging. I love the whole process, and love hanging out with writers. They're invigorating! A couple of weeks ago, I was at a retreat at a Buddhist centre in Santa Cruz, and every single person was an unpublished, earnest, committed writer. They took themselves seriously. And so do I."

Social Innovators

Larry Brilliant is an M.D. and M.P.H., board-certified in preventive medicine, epidemiology and public health. His career in public health began when he was chosen to be part of a four-person international team that led the successful World Health Organization smallpox eradication program in India and South Asia in the '70s. Then he returned to the U.S. and created the Seva Foundation, a charitable organization that fights blindness in developing countries. Just as his peers were talking about retirement options, he was asked to help Google create google.org, the philanthropic arm of the company (he later became vice president and chief philanthropic evangelist for the firm). In 2009, on his 65th birthday, he was named president of the Skoll Global Threats Fund, established by former eBay president and billionaire philanthropist Jeff Skoll, to tackle such issues as climate change, water scarcity and pandemics.

When I met Larry, none of this impressive history was on show. He greeted me with a bear hug, and his quick laugh and round belly made him seem more like my slightly kooky uncle from California than one of *Time* magazine's "100 most influential people." But his glowing example got me thinking.

According to traditional life-stage models, "giving back" is something we feel the urge to do as we grow older. We might go into politics, sit on the board of a local non-profit or offer our services to an international charity. Ripe pioneer Kelly McDougald says this is the message she got early in her career, when she started working in the technology sector. "I met someone who was about to retire, and he told me, 'There are three stages in life: you learn, you earn and then you return.' He was leaving corporate life and moving into philanthropy."

Times have changed. Today, many of us want our work to be the way we do good. All kinds of people—in every field and each sector—are finding ways to put the skills acquired in their careers to work on the world's greatest challenges. "We're now realizing," Kelly continued, "That we can do all three at the same time, in one role."

Barbara Johnson, 59, from publishing executive to social entrepreneur

"When I turned 50, I took a year off. I'd had a great career. After university, I became assistant city editor of the Dallas Morning News. *One day, Clay Felker, a New York editor who owned* Esquire *for a while and started* New York *magazine, called me. I was dazzled. At the time, he was at Adweek. I told him that didn't interest me, but he insisted that my scepticism would serve me well as editor. I took the job.*

Clay left Adweek the next year and introduced me to another protégé, Steve Brill. Steve and I started Texas Lawyer, then I became COO of American Lawyer Media. I was president of the company that started Court TV. Then launched two Internet companies, one with [marketing guru] Seth Godin, which we sold to Yahoo.

It all collapsed when the dot-com bubble burst in 2000. I celebrated my 50th birthday, and decided to take time off to think about what I would do next.

I found I loved being at home with my son. And while I was reasonably comfortable financially, I knew I had too much energy not to work. But it was also clear I needed to do something different. Completely different. I didn't want to do anything I'd done before. I didn't want to raise money. I didn't want it to be all about money, period.

So, I started talking to everyone I knew, including my sister, who introduced me to Pleasant Rowland, the founder of

American Girl [a company that makes hugely popular dolls and accessories, which was bought by Mattel for $700-million].

When we met, Pleasant told me about a program she had developed in the 1970s, designed to help children become better readers. It was successful but dormant while she built American Girl to great heights. Together, we decided it was time to bring it back.

Here's why. In America, two-thirds of fourth and eighth graders cannot read at grade level. This is not a workforce that will thrive in our new world.

So, we launched the Superkids Reading Program, invested millions revising Pleasant's original work, including research to ensure it worked in real classrooms—modern classrooms—creating the materials, and getting the organization up and running.

Our mission is to improve reading ability by the end of Grade 2. And we're accomplishing it by behaving like any for-profit educational publisher—we've hired a small army of sales people, we have a professional development team. We are competing to have schools buy our reading program. Because it's unquestionably more effective.

I now work with the kindest people I've ever known—thoughtful and humble, they give credit instead of seeking it. And it's wonderful to be part of an enterprise that is making a difference for the kids who most need champions."

• • •

The energy and enthusiasm of Pathfinders is thrilling—and contagious.

Now that you've met some Masters and Pathfinders—and have done some thinking and reflection about your own experiences and passions—we move to the next stage. In Week

Nine, we bring it all together to answer the big question that propels your journey, "What's next?"

Journal

• Have you been thinking about becoming a Pathfinder? Does it meet an urge you've had, but haven't been able to put into words? Does one of the three paths I've identified appeal?

Have you wondered what it would be like to work for yourself? Do you have an idea for a new venture? Or, would you like to follow your creative bent? Have you been working away in your atelier (whether basement or garage) for years, as painter Doris McCarthy did? Do you suddenly have an urge to pick up some clay or buy a drum kit? Perhaps you feel the pull to do good—would you like to ensure that your ripening helps other people and our planet?

Spadework

1. Is there something you've always wanted to do but never had the time, ability, courage or freedom to try? What is it? Do you feel ready to do it now?

2. As you read this chapter, did other Pathfinder role models come to mind? People you know? People you've heard about? What do their stories mean to you?

3. Revisit what you wrote about yourself in Week Three, when you answered the question, "Describe what it feels like to be you right here, right now." Is your answer still appropriate? How would you change it?

4. Reread your Ripe Principles (what you believe) and Ripe Credo (how you translate belief into action). Do both still fit? How might they need to change to match your evolving sense of yourself?

⟲ At any point in the journey, you can go back and review earlier weeks.

Week 1 • 2 • 3 • 4 • 5 • 6 • 7 • **8** • 9 • 10 • 11 • 12

The Pathfinders — Do you want to set out in a new direction?

Week Eight in Review

• Reinvention holds huge appeal. Many of us have dreams we'd like to achieve.

• Discover where the passion that seizes Pathfinders comes from.

• Consider what it would be like to work for yourself. In the U.S., the average first-time entrepreneur is now 55 to 64.

• Think about exploring your own creative impulse.

• Determine whether you feel the call to make a difference.

WEEK NINE:
Ripe Role

*"Be true to that which exists inside yourself
and thus make yourself indispensable."*
- André Gide

What's on the horizon?
Find the answer to the question "What's next?"

John Elkington, 60, from entrepreneur to innovative thinker

"My father's vision of my future would have been for me to be in the air force or become a merchant banker.

I went to university to study economics. A year later, in 1968, I gave up—it seemed to have little to do with what was happening on streets around the world. I took up sociology and social psychology instead, then did a post-graduate degree in urban planning.

But I didn't practice any of these once I got into the real world. I was extraordinarily lucky in meeting people who gave me a sense of direction. At 11, I'd raised funds to help the World Wildlife Federation in its first year. After graduation, I met Max Nicholson, one of its founders. Each of the conversations I had in those early days shaped how I view the world in a way my formal education did not.

Over the next three decades, I started three companies: Environmental Data Services, Sustainability, and Volans, each of them more progressive than the last. When I think about what I've done, the one thing that stands out is my contribution to the language. In 1984, I coined the term 'environmental excellence.' In 1986, 'green consumer.' Not long after, I started talking about 'sustainability.' For years, no one knew what I was saying, and I was forever defining and spelling it. And, of course, 'triple bottom line.' When I hit on that, I realized my education was playing out at last. There was an economic piece, a social piece and an environmental-planning piece.

My career has been a series of happy accidents. I met people, we decided to do things, and one thing led to another.

Volans is my current project, a venture I founded with Pamela Hartigan [director of the Skoll Centre for Social

*Entrepreneurship at Oxford University's Said Business School].
We're developing innovative solutions to financial, social and
environmental challenges, working with global firms at the
strategic and board level.*

*I intend to work until I drop. I feel as if I'm only beginning to
understand what it is I'm meant to be doing. Max Nicholson was
in his 70s when I met him and we worked together until he died
at 98. There's a great reservoir of experience in our aging
population and we've got to work out how to tap into that."*

At this point in your journey, everything you've been
discovering, doing and dreaming about begins to coalesce.

Let's pause for a moment. Take a deep breath. And think
about how far you've come. By Week Nine, you have increased
your understanding of what you have to offer. You have a
deeper sense of who you are and what you want from your
work. You've worked hard and been courageous. Bravo!

Now it's time to answer the question that drives your quest
—how will you ripen? What is the thing you will do? What will
your Ripe role be? (If you like the math metaphor, you're
completing the equation [experience + passion = ripening].)

Some Ripe pioneers had the good fortune of being offered
a new opportunity. Remember Larry Brilliant, who was named
president of the Skoll Global Threats Fund on his 65th
birthday? And Lisa Bayne, who was recruited to be the CEO of
Artful Home? Others seem to simply stumble upon it. Andrea
Knight, managing editor of the Azreili Holocaust Survivor
Memoirs, started asking people if they knew of any
opportunities, and educator Beverly Caswell spotted an

advertisement. Both knew immediately those opportunities were what they wanted to do next, and each of them used the same phrase when describing their "aha!" moment to me —"That's my job!" Others *knew* what their work would be. Laurie Orlov, founder of Aging in Place Technology Watch said her initial insight—there was an opportunity—was quickly followed by another thought, "Someone had to do it. I could. So, it should be me."

Having clarity at this stage is wonderful—and rare. Most of us need to continue to search for the answer. It's not unlike earlier in our working lives. Most of us didn't choose our first career—we fell into it or it was chosen for us. It's a refrain I heard from virtually every Ripe pioneer. As John Elkington said in his story at the beginning of this chapter, "My father's vision of my future would have been for me to be in the air force or become a merchant banker." (And before we feel too smug, it's a tradition that continues today. Reeve Carney, the young star of the Broadway musical "Spider-Man: Turn Off the Dark," says his parents tried it on him. "They used to whisper 'doctor' and 'lawyer' in my ear when I was sleeping, because they were both musicians and wanted me to have an easier life than they had.")

If you still don't know what your Ripe role will be, don't worry. This chapter will help you decide.

In fact, there a myriad of possible Ripe roles—from artist to academic, from clergy to entrepreneur. As you now realize, there are many, many ways in which to ripen.

How can you find your place in this exciting new movement? You need to come at this question from every angle. If it's not clear whether you want to be a Master and stay on the same path, or a Pathfinder and head in a new direction, set that aside for now.

Back in Week Four, I posed a number of questions. We're

going to think them through together again—with a difference. Earlier, you used them to expand your thinking. This week, they help you narrow the search and decide.

So, think about scope. Do you want a big challenge or a small one? Think about pace, too. Do you want to work really hard or slow down? Also consider whether you'd rather be inside an organization or working on your own. What about the work itself? Do you want to express yourself, build things, plan or innovate? Think about the outcome as well. Do you want to add to knowledge? Help people? Move them? Change the world?

As you move through this week—and its round of questions —your answers can start to be more specific. What kind of work? Which organization? Where?

Choosing your Ripe role is a critically important decision. It will require thought, for sure. But you also need to bring your whole self—and all of your resources—to the task at hand. Here are three approaches that worked for Ripe pioneers.

Creative

For nine weeks you've been on a creative journey. The first weeks were about the divergent part of the process—gathering information and gaining insight. This is the convergent part— where you connect the dots and begin to see something new taking shape. You're looking for threads and themes that run through your life and your ripening journey. What comes up again and again? What stands out?

What kinds of creative exercises can help you move ahead? When I work with clients, instead of just talking about what they might do, we imagine an ideal day. We walk through it together, seeing what they're doing, who they're with, and even what their workspaces look like. And we often do it in a physical way—they get up and walk around their chair, stand beside it or sit on the floor, anything to help them see themselves, and their future, in a fresh way.

You'll recall Lee Weinstein, the corporate refugee who started his own PR firm, used a similar—and wonderfully creative—approach to great effect. "After everything I'd done, I still wasn't sure what my work would be. So, I decided to do some free writes every morning and come up with different scenarios. The only rule I made for myself was that I had to write as long as I could, and without correcting or stopping. Stream of consciousness."

As you brainstorm, I encourage you to have big, bold thoughts. That's essential to the creative process—and universal among Ripe pioneers. Just as research for this book began, I read that Liza Minnelli, at 63, believed her "greatest contribution was yet to come." It makes sense, doesn't it? We're at the height of our powers and moving in new directions. There's great potential for us to do the kinds of things we only dreamed of. (This is not, as it's been called, an "encore" career. This is the main event.)

I was so taken with Liza Minnelli's bold assertion that I repeated it to everyone I interviewed and asked what they thought. Kelly McDougald responded enthusiastically: "Heaven help us if we don't feel that way! I see this parade of friends and colleagues ahead of me, thriving and making a contribution in new engagements. So, yes!" Lisa Bayne seconded her emotion, "Oh, I couldn't have put it better. I feel like I'm just hitting my stride." And John Elkington summed up how many of us are feeling, "Absolutely, I feel I'm only beginning to understand what it is I'm meant to do."

Finally, as you draw on your creative abilities, reach out to others. You're looking for constructive insights from people who care about you, including your Ripe Circle and Ripe Kitchen Cabinet, but also new people you've met along the way. What have they observed? When are you at your most passionate? Most authentic? When do you appear to lose track of time? See if they can shed light on the most creative challenge of your career.

Critical Thinking

Hello, critical self. Since Week Four, when we entered into a period of reflection and exploration, you've been waiting patiently in the wings for your chance in the spotlight. And this is it!

Critical thinking played a vital role in the decision-making process of Ripe pioneers. As they discovered, thoughtful analysis can help us move from dreaming to reality.

It's essential to critically assess what you've learned about yourself—your skills and strengths, your values and desires. Go back over your journal and the summaries at the end of each chapter to refresh your memory. And pay careful attention to what you've learned about the marketplace when you went reconnoitering in Week Six.

The best piece of advice author and management consultant Peter Drucker gave me as I began my own midlife search was I would discover my life's work at the intersection of who I am and what the world is looking for. This is good career advice in general, but it's particularly relevant as we ripen. If we focus only on "Where are the jobs?," our satisfaction will suffer. Conversely, if we only ask, "What do I want?," we may discover that no one is interested. The Ripe role you're looking for is the one that hits the sweet spot.

This week, call on your Ripe Kitchen Cabinet to help you think through what you've learned and where you might go from here. Share your thoughts, what you've discovered and what's turning your crank. And discuss ideas that are emerging in you. As your advisory group, they can be incredibly practical, helping to refine your thinking. Lee Weinstein found this to be so. "I wanted this group to represent a cross section and to speak their truths, whatever they were. They were like a glass of cold water—asking hard questions that woke me up. There were incredibly useful as I thought about my options and moved forward with my new venture."

And while you're thinking things through, ask yourself, "Is it sustainable?" That is, is the work you have in mind something you can see yourself doing for years to come? And—as much as anyone can tell the future—will the world continue to welcome it? Choose Ripe work that has room to grow.

Deeper

People sometimes want me to tell them the answer. "What should I do?," they ask. You may be tempted to pose the same question to people you know, including those in your Ripe Circle and Ripe Kitchen Cabinet. If you do—and if they answer, which I hope they will not—accept their input with thanks. Then turn back toward yourself. The only person who can answer this question is you.

The good news is the answer is inside of you, waiting to be discovered. I hope you will call on your psyche to help you decide. Yes, we need to do critical thinking, but we also need to check in with our gut. As you've already discovered, our inner GPS sees things our conscious mind does not. Why not invite this deep, knowing self to help you find your way?

Many Ripe pioneers realized their decision-making process wouldn't be entirely conscious, and many of them entered into a period of active reflection with trained professionals. Lee

Weinstein, Lisa Bayne and Murray Kelley all went into therapy as they began to ripen to help them reflect and decide.

Others discovered as they established a connection with their deepest selves, the way forward became clear. Remember Lynn Mizono from Week Five? A bad case of sciatica kept her housebound for six months, and being "forced into a state of being" gave her the insight and courage to sell her clothing design business and devote herself to art.

For many people, ripening is about connecting with our life's purpose. A number of men and women spoke movingly about having been called. "When Christians talk about vocation, they get a little apologetic," Phyllis Tickle laughed. The former academic and publishing executive, now an author who writes about her faith, said, "But, yes, this is my vocation in the fullest sense of the word. There are almost flashing lights that tell you where you're going next. And it is always a place where the natural talents you have and any skills you've developed are going to be used." (More on Phyllis Tickle and how she's living her beliefs in Week Eleven.)

• • •

Remember how you were feeling in Week One? What once seemed impossible is now taking shape. You are ripening.

If you know what your Ripe role will be, take some time to celebrate. Revel in it. And share your news with others. Lee Weinstein did it in a delightful way. "I didn't know what the business would be yet, but I was so sure of what was coming I called my mother right away and said, 'I'm going out to the gorge to start my own company.'"

After you've completed this week's reflections and spadework, if you're still not certain, don't despair. You're working toward the answer, but it can take time. Remember how we've talked about this being a circular path—that you may want to cross the same terrain more than once? If you don't have a clear sense of what your Ripe role will be, you might like to go back now and review some of the earlier chapters and reread your journal entries. (Be patient with yourself—there is room for everyone in this new world of work. Your answer will come!)

In Week Ten, we all take a giant step forward.

Journal

Which of the three decision-making paths we discussed this week appeal to you—creative, critical or deeper? Perhaps you'd like to do some work in all three areas, bringing your whole self and all of your resources to the task at hand.

• **Do you see it as a creative process?**
Try imagining yourself in a new role. Don't think about what it is just yet. Instead, explore what you're doing each day, who you're working with, where you work. Or try what Lee Weinstein did, and do a free write each morning. Start with a line such as, "I'm waking up and ..."

• **Would you like to do some critical thinking?**
What have you learned? What's going on inside of you? What's captured your imagination? And what is your Ripe sweet spot—the intersection of what you have to offer and what the world is looking for?

• **Or are you keen to engage with your deepest self once again?**
What insights does your psyche, gut or inner GPS have for you?

Spadework

1. Look back at Week One and reread your answer to the benchmark question, "What's next?" Is what you wrote still true? What's changed?

2. What is your Ripe role? If you don't know, write 10 possible answers as quickly as you can without stopping to reflect or correct.

3. What do you hear from others that might be helpful? Look for suggestions that reveal what people see in you, rather than what they may want for you. You're looking for something like, "Lori, did you know that your face lights up when you talk about …"

4. Do you have a clear sense of whether you want to continue on the familiar path (Master) or break new ground (Pathfinder)?

5. In Week Four, you made a drawing of yourself in a boat. Go back to that page in your journal and look at it with fresh (non-judgmental!) eyes. What do you see? Does this piece from the "right side" of your brain offer any insights about where you might be headed?

6. Try this exercise to help you create a role around an idea you might have. Draw a large circle. Write the idea or issue in the centre. Let's say it's "I love baby animals." Then, all around the circle, imagine what kind of role would help you connect with this passion. For instance, might you work for a non-profit organization that protects animal habitat? Or in government, creating legislation to do the same? What if you started a company that designs and manufactures products to protect fragile breeding grounds? What if you went into advertising and some of your clients do this kind of work? Or you go into cosmetics and ensure your company adheres to cruelty-free policies? Maybe you want to use it as a source of inspiration for a creative project—write a play or make videos. Perhaps you'll start a farm where innovative practices are nurtured. Or you become an eco-tour guide, helping to raise awareness. Just go with it, dream up as many possibilities as you can imagine. (And try this with as many variations as appeal to you. Try on a bunch of different hats!)

7. Does Liza Minnelli's statement resonate with you? Do you believe your greatest contribution is yet to come?

⟳ At any point in the journey, you can go back and review earlier weeks.

W e e k   1 • 2 • 3 • 4 • 5 • 6 • 7 • 8 • **9** • 1 0 • 1 1 • 1 2

Ripe Role — How will you answer the central question of your quest?

Week Nine in Review

- Complete the Ripe equation:
  [experience + passion = ripening].

- How will you ripen? What will your new work be?

- Some people are offered an opportunity, some just know
  what to do.

- Knowing is rare. Most of us need to continue the search.

- Be creative—connect the dots of your journey to see
  something new take shape.

- Is your greatest contribution yet to come?

- Critically assess what you've learned about yourself, your
  talents and what the world needs, and find the sweet spot.

- Call on your psyche—your inner GPS—to help you find your
  way.

WEEK TEN:
Ripe Know-How

"You must do the thing you think you cannot do."
- Eleanor Roosevelt

What's on the horizon?
Make the transition into your new Ripe role.

Susanne Ramirez de Arellano, 51, from journalist to explorer

"I was born and raised in Puerto Rico. My father told me, 'You've got to go out there and have a big career. Big, better, best: never let it rest until the big gets better, and the better best.'

I have more degrees than a thermometer. And had a great career as a journalist, with UPI, ABC News when Peter Jennings was there, with Reuters—and then with a Latin American news network.

I was commuting between this big, new job and New York City, involved in a new relationship, and my daughter was heading off to university. It was exhausting. One day, I said, 'Enough!' I just had to make a full stop.

It's been four months since I walked away, and I've been working on a contract for the International Women's Media Foundation since then. It's a great fit for me, since so much of my journalism has been dedicated to women's issues. I'm writing like crazy, something I haven't done in years. I wrote a speech for Annette Bening to give at one of our events, and when I heard her speaking my words, not changing anything, knowing when and how to pause, I thought, 'She's good at this—and so am I!' I love storytelling.

At this stage of the championship, I'm looking back. I've been at the top of the ladder, and it's not what I want now. In fact, I have no idea who that woman was. My priorities are changing.

I'm asking myself, 'What would make Susanne happy now?' I know how to do so many things, and I have energy and so much I want to do. I have this sense my greatest work is still ahead of me.

I'm searching, and it's not easy. I feel like I'm crossing the desert, totally, completely alone. And all I want to do is look across to see a fellow traveller."

W e're encouraged to believe we are solo travellers through this life, competing with one another at every turn. As we move into this new phase (heavy as it is with "U3" messages), is it any wonder we imagine ourselves to be alone?

Now you know this is not so. By Week Ten, you've read about many people who have ripened—and, no doubt, have noticed others around you. And let's not forget about your Ripe Circle and Ripe Kitchen Cabinet, who may be ripening along with you or preparing for their own journey.

Whether or not you've decided on a clearly-defined new role, you've realized you can do something new. This may be the first time you've said, "This is what I want and I'm going for it!" And, if you're like most Ripe pioneers, you're going to have to work hard to make your move. (The early stages of the ripening process are like chocolate. And, now we've arrived at the broccoli chapter. Sigh. You knew it was coming.)

In Week Two, we talked about how your journey would require thought and analysis, exploration and reflection. This is where the last bits—courage and persuasion—kick in. This week will help you figure out how to bring your new story to life. How to make a successful transition to your Ripe role. One part of your journey is coming to an end and a particularly crucial phase is just beginning.

Let's start by checking in with ourselves. As you contemplate moving beyond dreaming into action, what happens inside of you? For many of us, that inner pendulum we've been talking about on our journey—the one that swings between emotions like faith and doubt, elation and despair—really begins to move. Half the time you may feel certain about your new role and 100 percent committed to ripening. The rest of the time, you might feel scared to death, ready to give it all up and stay right where you are.

Takes us back to when we were starting out in our careers, doesn't it? When we felt awkward and wondered if we'd ever find our way. Of course, we're not tender fledglings now. We've been in the world for many years. And we have lots to offer as we set out into this new leg of the journey. (Plus, we're in good company. Changing jobs is the new normal. According to the Pew Research Center, "Fifty percent of employees have been with their current employer for less than five years.")

The way forward is different for everyone. And it is based on several factors—whether you're going to become a Master or Pathfinder, where on the continuum you'd like to be (be that a dramatic change or something familiar), and where you are in life, professionally and personally.

As you move through this transition, call on the loving, supportive energy of your Ripe Circle. Draw them close. They will cheer you on, pick you up if you stumble and celebrate your success. At the same time, the advisory capacity of your Ripe Kitchen Cabinet can kick into high gear. They'll help you think things through and prepare for you for what's coming—including "unknown unknowns" as former U.S. defense secretary Donald Rumsfeld famously put it—encouraging you to move forward in a different way.

What's Required?

Here's the big question to ask yourself this week: "What do I need to make a successful transition into my Ripe role?" In general, my clients and I talk about three core issues.

1. Your portfolio
What do you need in order to do this new work that's not in your portfolio now? A degree? Specific training? Field experience? Think about what's missing and how to get what you need.

2. Your life
Is everyone on side who needs to be? Have you been keeping your loved ones up to speed on your plans? Are you and your partner on the same page? (It's not uncommon for couples to want different things at this stage of life.) And have you considered the impact of changes to your benefit plan? Given she had a chronic illness, one client realized she would be unable to make a substantial change in direction until she'd reached official retirement age and could apply for government health-care insurance.

3. Your finances
I don't do financial planning, and refer my clients to people who do. But it's important to recognize money is an issue most people need to address.

Many Ripe pioneers continued with their original careers while building their new ones—author P.D. James is a great example. (This type of juggling is not uncommon to anyone who's earned an Executive MBA, for instance.)

We talk about sources of income—finding ways to finance the transition, including what was once called "moonlighting" and is now referred to as "alternative revenue streams." This is particularly critical if the work you're going to do isn't likely to generate much money. Artists, for instance, understand their passion may never earn much, so they need to find work that helps pay the bills. (I'm waiting for the day when the 70-year-old who served us lunch will be singing jazz standards in the lounge when we show up for cocktails that evening.)

We also discuss the option of downsizing. Author Rona Maynard says she and her husband moved from a "house-sized condo" to a compact loft when they agreed that a smaller, streamlined home would "expand their sense of possibility."

If financing issues slow you down, don't worry. Ripening isn't a time-limited offer—you don't have to make it happen right now. It's something you can do at 55, 65, 80 and beyond. In fact, coming back to this process is something you might want to repeat in the years to come. (We'll explore this together in Week Eleven.)

What's the Plan?

Everyone wants to know whether they should move forward methodically or just take a leap of faith.

Some people do make a dramatic change. You'll recall artist Lynn Mizono said she decided to "jump into the void." Most of us, however, need to carefully consider the variables. Which means we need some kind of plan.

Whether it's back-of-a-napkin or meticulous, a plan helps us articulate our vision, break it into actionable steps and establish a realistic timeline. This last part of the equation is particularly critical—the transitions to some Ripe roles happen very quickly, while others can go on for years. Playwright Rick Archbold framed his experience this way, "During the last 10 years of my freelance career, I was taking chunks of time to work on my own stuff. We had a cottage, and I would go up there for a week or two and just write."

As you plan, look for resources that will be helpful to you. For instance, lots of terrific organizations have popped up in the last few years to help entrepreneurs (including social innovators) find their way. Likewise, there are public and private institutions designed to help artists. And look for role models, too—who's doing what you have in mind, and what can you learn from their example? Last but not least (and this may come from your Ripe Kitchen Cabinet), look for a mentor. There will soon be more Ripe pioneers everywhere. In the meantime, people who have been serial reinventors can be extremely helpful. People like social media consultant Debbie Dimoff: "Because I've recrafted myself every few years throughout my career, I have a reputation as a reinventionist—they're always sending people to me who want to know how to get started."

One caution about planning: don't let endless variations of your Ripe plan stop your forward momentum. Planning is a favourite tactic of the procrastinator that lurks within each of us. Recognize that, and nip it in the bud.

What's Your Story?

Remember Laurie Orlov, founder of Aging in Place Technology Watch? When she decided to start her new venture, she realized the "if-you-build-it-they-will-come" model wasn't realistic. So, she figured out how to market her services: "Could I grow a business and gain credibility in a market without, say, a PR department like Forrester Research has, or sales reps or research associates? I decided I could. I give a lot of speeches, blog, and am often quoted in the press."

Figuring out how to sell yourself isn't new to most of us—everyone has applied for a job or tried to make a deal at some point in their careers. But when Ripe pioneers go public, a whole new level of persuasiveness is at work. Why? Because most of us will create our new work or encourage employers to reimagine it with us. In all cases, we need to be able to demonstrate the benefits of ripening—not just to us, but to the organization and to society in general. Kelly McDougald hit the nail on the head when she told me, "I call it the courage factor. The ability not only to envision yourself in a role, but to have the confidence to sell yourself in it."

One of my clients, a construction industry executive, was in his early 60s when his company was taken over. He struggled with whether or not to stay on, noting, "When I look around the table, everyone else is 20 years younger." One day, he called to say he'd made up his mind. He believed he had something to contribute and he could become a Master. Furthermore, he'd figured out what to say to his new CEO—he'd played a significant role in the success of the company in which they'd just invested, and he wanted to continue to do so. I could almost hear the grin spreading across his face when he said, "If it ain't broke, don't fix it."

Pathfinders face their own challenges. An entrepreneur may need to learn how to present to venture capitalists. Others might need to show why they're the ideal candidate for a job that has never before appeared on their CV. When Marilyn Grist was considering taking on the leadership of HelpAge USA, she thought carefully about why it made sense. "My mind started flashing to all of the things I'd experienced over 20 years with CARE. Of course old people can't run fast enough to get away from genocide! I was able to show—first to myself, and then to the organization—how all of my experience and this new challenge were connected."

· · ·

Jeff Fisher, a graphic designer who became a character clown in his 50s, repeated to me what his grandfather said to him, "Please tell me you'll never say, 'I should have.'" Words to live by.

You've seen it again and again throughout *Ripe*: rich, rewarding work is possible. And I know it's within your reach. You are ready to enter the next, best phase of your career.

Take a big breath, hold your head high and show the world what it means to be 50-plus today. What it means to ripen.

In Week Eleven, we'll think together about the years to come.

Journal

How are you feeling about the shift from "chocolate" to "broccoli?" Are you ready to move out into the world? Does the very thought thrill you to bits? Do you feel overwhelmed? How can you call on others (such as your constantly faithful Ripe Circle and Ripe Kitchen Cabinet) to help you make this important transition?

• What's required?
Do you have the capabilities and qualifications you'll need? What has the response been from the other important players—is everyone in your life on the same page? And have you thought how will you manage your finances?

• What's the plan?
Create a plan that defines your vision, the steps you need to achieve it and a timeline. As you do, keep writing in your journal. It will help you clarify where you're headed, what else you might need, and how to keep going through this challenging stage.

• What's your story?
Do you feel ready to make the case for why you're the best person to do this work—and worth investing in? (If not, the first exercise in this week's Spadework can help.)

Spadework

1. Let's practise making the case. Complete the sentences below that apply to your Ripe role. Do it spontaneously at first without too much thought, and see what comes. Then, carefully think through what you might say and how to put it—taking care to articulate and emphasize what you have to offer.

"I'm the ideal candidate for this job because ... "
"My services will help you ... "
"Investing in this new venture is a smart move for these reasons ..."
"This idea will help change the world in one important way ..."
"Collectors like you tell me my sculpture really speaks to them ..."

2. Do you feel ready to move into your Ripe role? If not, what else can you do to prepare?

3. Remember to update your resume as well as your profile on social-media sites such as LinkedIn, incorporating all the skills, strengths and other insights from your ripening journey.

4. What resources exist to help you make the transition? Are there organizations? Sources of funding? Role models?

5. Celebrate. We honour passages from one stage of life to another—birthdays, graduations, marriages. Why not create a ceremony to celebrate your ripening? Make it something private or throw a party and invite all your friends. It can be a great way to say thank you to your Ripe Circle and Ripe Kitchen Cabinet, too.

At any point in the journey, you can go back and review earlier weeks.

W e e k   1 • 2 • 3 • 4 • 5 • 6 • 7 • 8 • 9 • 10 • 11 • 12

Ripe Know-How — What do you need to put in place so you can ripen?

Week Ten in Review

- We are not alone on this journey—some people have already ripened, and many more are in the process.

- How do you make the transition from dreaming to doing?

- What's required? What experience or training or space do you need?

- Is your personal life in order? Are your loved ones on board?

- Have you considered your financial status? How will you keep money coming in?

- Create a plan that articulates your vision, breaks it into actionable steps, and establishes a realistic timeline.

- Think carefully about how to make your case—whether to your employer, an investor or potential client.

- Rich, rewarding work is within reach!

WEEK ELEVEN:
Ripe, Plus

"The old woman I shall become will be quite different from the woman I am now. Another I is becoming."
- George Sand

What's on the horizon?
Look toward the years ahead and anticipate your future.

Murray Kelley, 65, from modern dancer to early childhood educator

"I did the typical Boomer thing, 'I don't need a profession yet, I'll do a liberal arts degree.' Then, I went to Africa and taught English for two years in Sierra Leone.

My father was a United Church minister and he had the same kind of academic ambitions for me. So I spent seven years studying theology at the University of Edinburgh and the University of Toronto.

In the mid-'70s, I abandoned my PhD and started dancing. I came out, too–late, at 28. For the rest of the '70s, I travelled to New York every six months or so to take modern dance classes. I realized I was really far behind. Most dancers start as children–I was 30.

I moved to New York to study with Merce Cunningham. There were a lot of independent choreographers also studying there, so I got work. And I cleaned houses to survive.

In 1991, when I turned 46, I realized my dance career was coming to an end, and I needed to explore other interests. I took two MA degrees in New York–one at Bank Street College of Education in infancy and early development, the other in social work at Columbia.

At 50, I started working at Bank Street College, which is a small, progressive graduate school. In the last 15 years, I've done a range of things, and it's been completely engrossing work.

As I looked back, I began to see threads running through my life. For instance, while I was in Edinburgh, I took a couple of dance classes and volunteered at the Royal Hospital for Sick Children. At the time, the threads didn't seem to be related, but some part of me knew I wanted to dance, and some part of me knew I wanted to work with children.

Two years ago, I took a sabbatical and spent the year writing a theoretical reflection on the foundations of progressive education and the inclusion of children with special needs.

This year, I turn 65. I'm fortunate because my job can continue to evolve. Most recently, I've taken on a lot of supervising—therapists, teachers in speech, in special ed. There's a lot of reflective work and the unpredictable nature of it means it's always interesting.

At 73, I'll be entitled to a second sabbatical. But I don't see myself stopping work completely. In fact, going into therapy 20 years ago helped me find this work, and I've recently gone back to work with the same therapist to contemplate the chapter that lies ahead. To think about what shape it might take."

To some, working beyond 65 may seem unnatural and carrying on into our 70s positively outré. But soon, according to the World Health Organization, holding a job on our 100th birthday won't be unusual. John Beard, director of the WHO's Department of Aging and the Life Course, says most people born in developed countries today can expect to live well past 100, with the onset of disabling illness delayed close to the end of life. "This means we'll be working into our 70s, 80s and beyond," he says.

Does that sound far-fetched? In fact, it's already happening. According to the RAND Corporation, 17 percent of American men and women aged 65 to 75 were in the workforce in 1990. Since then, the number has jumped to 25 percent, and a significant rise in employment among those older than 75 was also seen.

What's more, RAND researchers project a sharp increase in these figures in the next decade.

Do you intend to work forever? I asked each Ripe pioneer this question. Some talked about a finite period, as in "another 10 years." Others were uncertain. Social innovator Rosa Lee Harden said she'd recently seen her good friend, Phyllis Tickle, who at 77 continues to write and give speeches around the world. "I confided to her I was thinking of doing one more thing before I retired. 'Retire?' she laughed. 'You're 55. What are you talking about?'"

The vast majority of Ripe pioneers said they will always work. They're not just postponing retirement, but eliminating it as an option altogether. In this, they echo many of the high-profile people who are on this journey with us—can you imagine Barbra Streisand, Robert Redford or Christopher Plummer coming to a complete stop? As Peter Frampton recently told Oprah Winfrey, "The 'R-word' isn't even in my vocabulary."

It's something Jerry Morris believed wholeheartedly. Just after the Second World War, he led a study to examine heart-attack rates in different occupations in England. The results showed a striking difference in transit workers—sedentary drivers were more than twice as likely to die of a heart attack as the conductors who went up and down 500 steps a day.

Morris proved exercise helps you live longer. And it worked for him. At 99, he was still making his way each day to his office at the London School of Hygiene and Medicine, and lobbying government to encourage people to take up regular physical activity.

What does Morris's example tell us? Aside from underlining the importance of keeping fit, it reminds us we need to think about our future selves—what we might need in the years after our initial ripening. In Week Nine, I wrote,

"There are many, many ways in which to ripen." Here, I'll add, "and many, many years in which to do it."

As we move into our 70s, 80s and beyond, the terrain changes. How do we navigate the new landscape and continue to ripen?

When I'm 64

As we've talked about, 50 is an important hinge-point in a Baby Boomer's life—when we realize we need to find a way to rejuvenate our work. And 65 is an equally important birthday.

Let's look ahead together. Imagine you've chosen a Ripe role for yourself, and worked hard to make the transition. After you've been at it for a while—Ripe pioneers talk about two or thee years, sometimes five—it's good to lift your head, look around and reassess. (Remember what I. Garrick Mason said in Week Two about heading for the lighthouse and course correcting from time to time?) You'll need to ask yourself, is the work you chose for this phase of your working life what you had in mind? Is it still working for you? Does it fit in all the right ways— putting your experience into play while stretching you in new directions? This includes people who become Masters—if you decided to stay on the same path, are you continuing to ripen? Or is it time to change?

If we choose well, and if our work is sustainable, we can continue and bloom in new ways. Sister Sheila Devane, of the Medical Missionaries of Mary, found this to be true. "Sixty-five feels like a turning point for me. So, after 40 years as a medical missionary in Africa, I've returned to Ireland to be with the sisters and reflect. I'll continue working in mental health [something she took up at 50], but now I feel called to work here at home."

If you discover at, say, 65, you're not feeling fully satisfied, if the work you've been doing has come to an end, if you're looking for a new challenge, or if the game has changed around you, it might make sense to take a second trip along the ripening path. You'll be able to look at what you wrote the first time you passed this way and explore what's different.

I recently worked with a woman in her early 60s who'd had an interesting and deeply satisfying career, and was eager to talk about what she might do next. One day, a new level of awareness about the pattern of her work dawned on her. She looked at me and said, "I've been in the shadows of a series of large personalities." Now, she wanted to be the star of her own show.

When choosing a Ripe role, people often make what is a natural and relatively easy first step, later moving into something that is more of a stretch. When we met author Rona Maynard in Week Two, she talked about stepping down in her 50s from a high-profile editor's job and writing her autobiography. In her 60s now, Rona has created a series of workshops to teach women how to tell their own stories—and is on the lookout for the next big challenge. She fully intends to continue ripening, and cites her mother as a powerful role model: "I watched my mother in her 50s and 60s. She was of that generation of highly-educated and gifted women who couldn't get into the salaried workforce because they were female. An academic, she had to give up her first job when she was pregnant with me, so she created her own career as a writer, a speaker and broadcaster. All through middle age, she was working on things. She died when she was 67, but I have no doubt she'd have kept going into her 80s."

Riper

When I asked social innovator Barbara Johnson, 59, if she would work forever, she replied, "I have another two incarnations in me." While Barbara reports being fully engaged at the Superkids Reading Program, she is also looking toward the horizon.

When she said that, I thought about the notion of legacy, and how it has always made me cringe. For me, it's not about what happens when we're gone—ripening is about living fully as long as we live. French novelist George Sand put it beautifully: "Try to keep your soul young and quivering right up to old age, and to imagine right up to the brink of death that life is only beginning. I think that is the only way to keep adding to one's talent, to one's affections, and to one's inner happiness."

In Week Four, I mentioned a survey that shows we are least happy at 50. On a happier note, our psychological well-being increases steadily after the mid-century mark and peaks in our 80s. (The graph is below.) And that's just the way things stand

The Happiness Graph

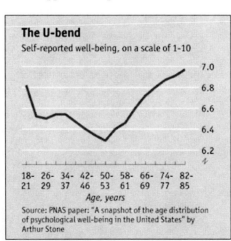

The Economist, December 16, 2010

today—I fully expect these numbers to change again as we ripen (as we continue to work, might happiness peak earlier? Or later? Or just continue on a high?).

In an article in *Psychology Today*, psychiatrist James Gordon, a professor at Georgetown University School of Medicine, recalled having dinner with painter Robert Rauschenberg (then in his 80s). "After we finished eating, Rauschenberg said it was time to get back to work. My friend asked him if he ever took time off. 'Honey, I don't want more time off. I want more time on.'"

What do you want to be doing in your 70s, 80s and beyond? Will you continue as a Master? Will you become a master of the thing that was once unfamiliar to your 50-something self? Or will you be ready to try something completely different?

One of the interesting things about our later Ripe years is Pathfinders become Masters. Remember Doris McCarthy whose career as a painter began when she retired from teaching? When I was in my mid-40s and Doris had just entered her 10th decade, I went to one of her openings. As the artist and I stood together in front of an oil painting of an iceberg made while on a recent trip to the Arctic, I asked how long it had taken to create. "A lifetime," she replied.

Masters become Pathfinders, too. I'm thinking of businessman Sidney Harman who bought *Newsweek* the year he turned 91, a departure for this audio-equipment magnate. And then there's Kye Marshall, 65, a jazz composer and music psychotherapist who is developing a new reputation for her lyrical, colourful photography.

There's also Phyllis Tickle, 77. "I started out as an academic, then ran St. Luke's Press. At 59, I quit, saying, 'It's time to do what I want,' which was to be a writer. A year later, Publisher's Weekly asked me to set up a department of religion.

At 70, I realized that the commercial lens wasn't nearly as interesting to me as the theology—booksellers are only interested in sales and all I wanted to talk about were the breathtaking ideas. I wanted to put on my baseball cap that says, 'I'm a Christian!' Since then, I've been writing and speaking publicly with real pleasure and joy. And now, in my late 70s, I'm experiencing a period of restlessness. Something's going to change again, but I don't yet know what."

Authenticity

I've found being in my 50s to be dramatically different from the rest of my adult life—I'm not the same physically or psychologically. You'll recall I asked Ripe pioneers if life after 50 was different for them, too, and their replies were a chorus of "Yes!" (It's not that "60 is the new 40," but more "This is what 60 is like now.")

I find myself watching older people with great curiosity, especially those who are at the height of their powers—or were when they died—like sculptor Louise Bourgeois, Indian prime minister Indira Gandhi, South African prime minister Nelson Mandela, violinist and conductor Yehudi Menuhin, and photographer Irving Penn.

Let's think about this together. If we change at 50 and 65, surely 80—or 100—will be different again. Remember when we discussed the "acorn theory" in Week Five? Might this be that process in reverse? Instead of expansion, are we being distilled to our essence? Our truest selves? Is that the work that will be before us at this stage?

Phyllis Tickle seems to suggest this, when she said she wanted to be able to "wear the baseball cap that says 'I'm a Christian.'" She also noted it's not because time is running out. "No, it's not that. It's just what I'm meant to do is just crystal clear now." And, at 60, playwright Rick Archbold appears to be headed in that direction, too. "The trajectory of my writing has become more and more personal. I started 3,000 years ago with the Odyssey. Then I wrote about a gay couple living in the 1940s and '50s. Now, I'm writing a play about a gay couple who are like me and my partner. I'm more courageous, perhaps. Certainly more willing to get to the centre of things."

It seems to me this distillation is the most desirable outcome of this entire process—we discover who we truly are and live that to the full.

That is ripening.

• • •

Are we ever fully ripe? That's for each of us to decide. My wish is for us to see ripening not just as an end goal—but as an ongoing process that continues for the rest of our lives.

This is the end of the individual part of the ripening process, yet your journey is just beginning. No doubt you will continue to grow, to learn and to do. To fully become who you are. And meant to be.

And the world will be better for it. Let's explore this idea together in Week Twelve.

Journal

• When I'm 64

Imagine how you might feel a few years into your ripening. And consider what you might want and need at that stage—perhaps you'll want to take the entire journey over again. Or spend time in the chapters or the Spadework that feel most appropriate to you.

Of course, I hope you'll keep *Ripe* nearby so you can do this at any point—two years, three years, five years from now.

• Riper

Now, imagine yourself 10, 20, 30 or more years from now. What will you be looking for? Come back to the Ripe journey from time to time, perhaps as you reach major milestone birthdays.

• Authenticity

Do you know people who have been distilled to their essence? How will you deepen your ripening?

Above all, keep writing in your journal so you stay connected to your authentic self—and to this process.

Spadework

1. Do you intend to stop work someday? Why? Why not? When? Do the people in your life expect you to?

2. Who are your role models for people working past 65? Newsmakers? People you know? Men and women from history?

3. How do you feel about the Ripe process coming to an end? What can you do to stay connected to it? To remain in contact with the new people you've met, or the people in your Ripe Circle and Ripe Kitchen Cabinet? Might you also keep your guiding Ripe Principles and your actionable Ripe Credo close at hand?

At any point in the journey, you can go back and review earlier weeks.

Week 1 · 2 · 3 · 4 · 5 · 6 · 7 · 8 · 9 · 10 · **11** · 1 2

Ripe, Plus — What will you be looking for when you reach 65 or 80?

Week Eleven in Review

- Do you intend to work forever?

- There are many years in which to ripen.

- As you turn 65, you might want to revisit the ripening process to ensure your new role is still on track.

- In fact, check back on milestone birthdays to see if you need to do something new.

- Painter Robert Rauschenberg, then in his 80s, was asked if he ever takes time off. He replied, "I don't want more time off, I want more time on!"

- Consider what happens as we grow older—are we distilled to our essence?

WEEK TWELVE:
Ripe Society

"This will be the decade when the cognitive map of aging gets redrawn. We will realize the blessings and benefits of later-life work."
- Harry Eyres, *Financial Times*

What's on the horizon?
Imagine how your ripening might change the world.

As Week Twelve begins, think back to the people you've read about who have taken up challenging new work in their 50s, 60s—and later. Each of them broke away from the "U3" chorus to sing a new song. Each is a vital, creative contributor.

Ripening is good news for people like us—over and over those who blazed the path told me, "This is the most satisfying work I've ever done." But is it just the icing on the cake of our careers? Or is there more to the story?

When Ripe pioneers said they truly believe their "greatest contribution" is still to come, they weren't talking exclusively about their own ambitions. Yes, they are pursuing their agendas, but each also sees their work as contributing in some way to the greater good.

Sitting at my desk, I reflected on these conversations and wondered: might our inner adventurer lead us into uncharted territory—not just as individuals, but as a society? What if we were to work together to create a world in which there was no time limit on individual achievement? A world where people—without exception—were encouraged to continue to develop and share their unique gifts with others?

Here are some of the ideas that came to me as I wrote *Ripe*. Let's use them to start a world-changing conversation—one that leads to lasting change.

Let's Put Out the Fire

Before we do anything, we need to stop the fire that's burning—before it becomes a conflagration.

What fire? It may not be obvious to all, especially those who've done well in life, but we are witnessing the birth of a new class—the involuntarily retired. *The New York Times* reported, "according to the U.S. Labor Department, 2.2 million people over the age of 55 were out of work in October 2010." Many people 50 or older believe they will never work again. If we don't do something—and soon—they may not. And then we will have an even larger crisis on our hands.

We need to introduce programs that will protect jobs—and create new ones—for people 50-plus. Yes, affirmative action. And let's find innovative ways to do it so short-term solutions become part of a sustainable future.

Why not, for instance, make older workers part of the public infrastructure rebuilding process? The brilliant YouthBuild program in the U.S., which helps low-income youth from 16 to 24 work toward their high-school diplomas, learn job skills, and serve their communities by building affordable housing, is a perfect model. What about SeniorBuild? (This will help us stay "active and engaged"—two birds with one stone!)

Let's get business on board. Companies like Home Depot have already figured out employees older than 50 years of age are more knowledgeable and more willing to share what they know. It's abundantly clear Baby Boomers prefer to be served by others of their generation—the possibilities for customer-facing roles are endless.

And let's invest in services that give first-time entrepreneurs the help they need to get their ventures off the ground, and create work for themselves and jobs for others, too.

Let's Imagine the Future

After a Christmas lunch with a dear friend who is planning to retire, I walked home slowly, head down, deep in thought. I was troubled that he hadn't given much consideration to what he was going to do with the years ahead—his "third third" as it's sometimes called.

Suddenly, I stopped. There on the sidewalk before me lay a stick, blown down in the previous night's storm. Someone had stepped on it, breaking it into two pieces—one of the pieces was two-thirds of the full length, the other, one third. I laughed.

I wasn't just amused by the literal representation of what had been on my mind. The space between the two pieces of wood—the gap—caught my eye and ignited my imagination. "We need a gap year for grown-ups!," I cried out, and rushed to get back to writing.

As you know, a gap year is an established tradition for students—time between school and university spent traveling, working, "chilling." Why not introduce a similar break for everyone in their 50th year? A time to completely step away from our usual routines. We could spend our year in service, such as the Peace Corps. We could use it for study, writing or reflection. Whatever we choose, we would return refreshed and ready to ripen.

But why stop there? What if we were to create centres around the world where people like us could meet for their gap year? Imagine the subjects on offer, the conversations in the hallways, the new ventures that would emerge!

That's just one idea. In a broader sense, what exactly do I mean by "a world in which there is no time limit on individual achievement, where everyone is encouraged to continue to develop and share their unique gifts with others?" Let's start by recognizing the abundance of resources. As consultant John Elkington noted, "There is a great reservoir of experience in our aging population and we've got to work out how to tap into that." Let's look closely at the value of these contributors, and how best to deploy them. What, precisely, does this generation have to offer? What are employers and consumers looking for that ripened men and women are best able to deliver? And what are the roles for which we are ideally suited?

Then, let's create a system that encourages older workers to learn, grow and contribute. Training and education, certainly. But what about practical support (and funding) for Pathfinders, whether entrepreneurs or inventors, artists or social innovators? What about changes to workplaces that encourage—and enhance—ripening for Masters?

And let's not stop there. Let's rethink the entire culture so it honours and embraces its most mature (and maybe even wisest) members. How about encouraging collaboration (something the gap year will help to intensify)? Mentoring is just one example. By all means, encourage the existing model—elder statesman advises novice politician—but let's expand it to include peer to peer. Those of us who've done well can help others in our cohort realize their dreams—can you imagine a more powerful or significant journey than helping others find their way?

Let's create a vernacular. We need words to describe this new phase of our lives—an idiom that captures the spirit of what it means to be 50, 65 or 80 today. Like "ripe."

And recognition, please, lots of recognition. There are many programs and awards that honour young achievers. Let's see major sponsors step forward and shine a spotlight on Ripe pioneers. "Top 50 Over 50" would be a good start.

Let's Fulfill Our Destiny

Those of us born after the Second World War came of age at an amazing time—an era full of hope, a time of endless possibility, an age when we thought we could change the world.

In recent years, attacking Boomers for what we *haven't* done has become a popular blood sport. I find this disturbing (and wearying) for two reasons. First, because it's inaccurate. This generation pushed to end an unjust war, opened doors for women, gays and people of colour, and helped launch the environmental movement. All these things, as well as access to birth control and holistic medicine, along with freedom of religious choice, characterize the Baby-Boomer mindset. Second, the blame game is dreadfully demoralizing—why would Boomers try anything new when we know we're likely to be voted off the island by young people who want our jobs? The fact is, there's room for all of us. And it seems incredibly foolish to be dismissing us just as the world faces its greatest challenges—if there ever was a time for "all hands on deck," this is it.

This book began when I noticed a discrepancy between my experience and the ubiquitous messages about what it is supposedly like to be 50 and older. The same observation applies here. Let's ignore all that noise, and focus on something positive, constructive and hopeful instead. It's time to rekindle the embers that burn deep inside of us. To come full circle in our lives. As Baby Boomers, our greatest achievement will not only be what we do as individuals, but what we've always done best as a generation: redefine the boundaries of the possible.

• • •

For 12 weeks, we've been on a journey together. We've come a long way, and learned much about ourselves and our fellow travellers.

Of course, your Ripe journey is just beginning. As we discussed last week, it's not an end goal, but a process that can continue throughout our lives. "Ol' Blue Eyes" really did get it right when he sang "The Best is Yet to Come."

In the days and weeks ahead, keep this book close by, and refer to it when you have questions or doubts. Keep writing in your journal. And stay close to the people who helped make your journey possible, including me.

I know you're going to do wonderful things. And I hope you'll contact me to share your story, so I can pass it along and inspire others. hello@juliamoulden.com

Journal

- How do you feel now that you've reached this stage of your journey (not the end, but a milestone to be sure)?

Spadework

1. How will you stay connected to your inner GPS so you can continue to ripen? What can you do to help someone else begin this journey or resume it if they've run into difficulty? Will you become part of someone else's Ripe Circle or Ripe Kitchen Cabinet now? Have you considered mentoring someone?

2. How can you change your organization so it's Ripe-friendly? What can be done to help welcome and develop employees who are 50-plus?

3. What else might you do to help change the world?

4. If you haven't already done so, take time to thank your Ripe Circle and Ripe Kitchen Cabinet. Let them know how much you appreciate their support and advice.

At any point in the journey, you can go back and review earlier weeks.

Week 1 • 2 • 3 • 4 • 5 • 6 • 7 • 8 • 9 • 10 • 11 • **12**

Ripe Society – Imagine how your ripening might change the world.

Week Twelve in Review

- Let's change the world view of aging, work and retirement.

- Why not make older workers part of the public-infrastructure rebuilding process?

- Let's encourage businesses to embrace and utilize the experience of those 50-plus.

- How about a gap year for grown-ups?

- How about creating more programs to support ripening, including educational and financial?

- Let's recognize the achievements of Ripe individuals. "Top 50 Over 50" would be a good start.

- Let's do what Boomers do best—redefine the boundaries of the possible.

Voices of Experience

My deepest thanks to the Ripe pioneers—for breaking ground and inspiring us with their stories.

Lisa Bayne
artfulhome.com
Full profile, Page 51

John Elkington
volans.com
Page 125

Ellen Greene
ellengreene.com
Page 114

Marilyn Grist
helpageusa.org
Page 97

Gary Hirschberg
stonyfield.com
Page 95

Barbara Johnson
rowlandreading.com
Page 117

Murray Kelley
bankstreet.edu
Page 153

Andrea Knight
azreilifoundation.org
Page 79

Ira Levine
ryerson.ca
Page 37

Rona Maynard
ronamaynard.com
Page 21

Laurie Orlov
ageinplacetech.com
Page 112

Susanne Ramirez de Arellano
iwmf.org
Page 139

Catherine Thompson
fiain.ca
Page 100

Lee Weinstein
leeweinstein.biz
Page 65

I interviewed the following Ripe pioneers for this book and will share more of their stories in my *Huffington Post* column and on juliamoulden.com.

Rick Archbold, author and playwright
flagforcanada.ca, studio180theatre.com

Peter Bregg, photographer
peterbreggphotography.com,
photosensitive.com

Beverly Caswell, educator

Phil Cubeta, professor of philanthropy and blogger
theamericancollege.edu, gifthub.org

James Dawson, photographer
jamesdawsonphoto.com

Sister Sheila Devane,
Medical Missionaries of Mary
medicalmissionariesofmary.com

Debbie Dimoff, social media consultant

Jeff Fisher, graphic designer and character clown
jfisherlogomotives.com

Val Fox, director of digital-media incubator
digitalmediazone.ryerson.ca

Rosanne Freed, blogger
rosannefreed.wordpress.com

Liza Gross,
International Women's Media Foundation
iwmf.org

Rose Lee Harden, social innovator
lifechangeru.com

Bob Keteyian,
therapist and communications expert
eliasandketeyian.com

Kimberley Ann Kistler, holistic veterinarian
animal-heal.de

Veronika Litinski, Cogniciti
cogniciti.com

Betty Londergan, author and blogger
bettylondergan.com,
whatgives365.wordpress.com

Kye Marshall,
composer, music psychotherapist,
photographer
kyemarshall.com

I. Garrick Mason, editor
scope-mag.com

Kelly McDougald, Knightsbridge
knightsbridge.ca

Howard Nussbaum,
Defining Wisdom Project
wisdomresearch.org

Vicki Saunders, entrepreneur
vickisaunders.com

David Simms, Opportunity International
opportunity.org

Joel Solomon, Renewal Partners
renewalpartners.com

Alan Spinrad, lawyer and managing partner
samuelslaw.com

Marilyn Strong, death midwife
handsofalchemy.com

Kiki Tidwell, angel investor
northwestenergyangels.com

Phyllis Tickle, author
phyllistickle.com

Anne Van Burek, author and educator

Acknowledgements

One name appears on the cover of this book, but many people helped me give birth to it. I have the great fortune of being loved by a remarkable tribe.

Rick Archbold, without whom *Ripe* would still be a pile of papers. Trisse Loxley, who helped take it from first to final draft, was the best editor ever—smart, kind and hysterically funny.

Each member of my Ripe Circle and Ripe Kitchen Cabinet, all of them thoughtful advisors who have become lifelong friends, offered vital insights at a pivotal moments (and helped me keep the faith when all I wanted to do was quit!): Michelle and Tal Bevan, Debbie Dimoff, Rosanne Freed, Nancy Gipson, Andrea Knight, Hilary McMahon, Jaimie MacPherson, Larry Raskin, Will Smith, Louise Walker and Rick Wolfe.

Julia Howell astonished me by always knowing what the next move should be. Wendy Shaw and Jill Roussy helped me chose the right path forward, way back when. And Kye Marshall has helped me course-correct for many years.

Interns Anna Hirtenstein, Zachary Keuhner and Fan Li brought great ideas to the table and connected me to their equally-idealistic generation. PhD candidate Erin Bentley transcribed 24/7 and added thoughtful commentary as she did. Will Eagle got my social-media self off the ground. And Gloria Roheim and Ricardo McRae helped me learn to fly.

Arianna Huffington invited me to be part of her spectacular adventure (and connected me to people all over the world). And the Speakers' Spotlight team, who treat me like a princess, each and every time.

All of the Ripe pioneers who shared their stories. And my clients who choose me as their trusted partner.

My family, who never stopped believing and who gave me the energy and confidence to keep ripening.

And my three stepsons.

I bow deeply to each of you. Thank you for sharing this journey with me.

- Julia Moulden
  Toronto, February 2011

About the Author

Julia Moulden is an author, speaker and columnist.

She is known for her ability to spot emerging trends with *Ripe* as the latest example. Her three books have sold around the world, and been translated into four languages.

Julia now reaches thousands of people each week via the *Huffington Post*, where her popular column appears every Saturday. Over the course of her career, she has written for visionary leaders and their organizations, including speeches for CEOs, cabinet ministers and celebrities.

As a speaker, Julia is always in demand. People use words like "inspiring" and "unforgettable" to describe her presentations—she helps people change the way they think about their work and our world.

An autodidact, Julia has traveled the world, and lived in Europe, the U.S. and Mexico. She speaks rudimentary French, humble German and market Spanish. Toronto is home base, and she kayaks as often as possible on Georgian Bay.

LaVergne, TN USA
12 March 2011
219819LV00001B/26/P